1836 FACTS
ABOUT THE ALAMO
AND THE TEXAS WAR FOR INDEPENDENCE

Mary Deborah Petite

SAVAS PUBLISHING COMPANY
202 First Street S.E., Suite 103A
Mason City, Iowa 50401
For distribution call, (800) 732-3669

1836 Facts About the Alamo and the Texas War For Independence
by Mary Deborah Petite

Copyright © 1999
Mary Deborah Petite

Includes bibliographic references and index

Printing Number

10 9 8 7 6 5 4 3 2
First Edition (paper)
ISBN 1-882810-35-X

Savas Publishing Company
202 First Street SE, Suite 103A
Mason City, IA 50401
515-421-7135 (editorial offices)

Trade Distribution:

Stackpole Books
5067 Ritter Road
Mechanicsburg, PA 17055
800-732-3669

F
390
.P48
1999

This book is printed on 50-lb. acid-free paper. It meets or exceeds the guidelines for permanence and durability of the Committee on Production Guidelines for Book Longevity of the Council on Library Resources.

For Damian, Jordan, and Isaiah.

The Alamo. Taken in 1920, this photograph shows the chapel front as it appears today. U.S. Army troops added the rounded center in 1849. *National Archives*

TABLE OF CONTENTS

continued. . .

CONTENTS (continued)

PHOTOGRAPHS & MAPS

Introduction

Texas fever hit the United States in the 1820s. Hundreds of Americans headed for the Texas border, leaving behind their peculiar epitaph, G.T.T. "Gone to Texas,"scrawled on doors and proclaimed in letters. Driven westward by their quest for land and opportunity, they believed the Mexican province of Texas was a Promised Land, a place for new beginnings.

Mexico had undertaken an ambitious program of colonization in hopes of developing her vast stretches of empty territory. Laws of 1824 and 1825 invited foreigners to settle in Texas, where they could live free of taxes and exempt from customs duties. The colonist-agents, called empresarios, received huge grants of land in return for establishing colonies and bringing in settlers. Every family received 4,428 acres for about four cents an acre. Little was asked of the colonists in return; they were required to be of good character, to take the Mexican oath of allegiance and to promise to be at least nominal Catholics.

Between 1825 and 1830, United States citizens began flocking to Texas with or without permission. Unlike the colonists who had received land grants, these new arrivals felt little loyalty to Mexico. By 1830, Americans made up over 75% of the population. Mexico was going through a period of political unrest and although preoccupied with troubles at home, the Mexican government was growing increasingly fearful of the Anglo-American expansion in Texas. Mexico soon turned her full attention to the Texas settlers. On April 6, 1830, the Mexican congress passed a law forbidding further immigration from the United States. The new law suspended all unfilled colonization contracts, ended the colonists' monopoly on coastal shipping, banned future slavery, and required all foreigners to have passports issued by the Mexican Consulate at their place of residence. Most troubling of all, the colonists lost the duty exemption which Mexico had given them on essential goods and materials. By 1831, General Manuel Teran was stationing troops all over Texas to see that the new laws were enforced.

The Texians (as they preferred to call themselves) were incensed by the new law. They believed they had been guaranteed self-government under the Mexican Constitution of 1824, which was now being overturned in favor of "centralism." A War Party, nicknamed the "War Dogs," emerged among the Texians. The War Party saw no solution short of rebellion and independence. Of this group, none was more vocal than William Barrett Travis. From the start his heart was with the American colonists in the growing friction with Mexico.

A glimmer of hope appeared in 1832 with a new revolution in Mexico. The hostile President Bustamente was out, and the new leader was General Santa Anna, a professed liberal who seemed sympathetic to the Texians. As a sign of good faith, customs duties were lifted for another two years. Stephen Austin, the first empresario, had always believed in cooperating with the Mexican government and was committed to peace. Austin urged caution and patience. Texas had always been promised separate statehood as soon as it had enough people. Austin believed that the new liberal Mexican government would agree that the time was right. He went to Mexico City with a petition for statehood and a proposed constitution in the summer of 1833. Instead of an approval for statehood, Austin and his petition were met with evasion and delays, and he ended up imprisoned in Mexico City.

Trouble was brewing early in 1835. Once entrenched in power, Santa Anna turned into another anti-American dictator and was more hostile than ever. He slapped customs duties on the colonists and sent Captain Antonio Tenorio to Anahuac to see that the law was enforced. Santa Anna dissolved the local legislature and the representatives were placed under arrest. In August, Santa Anna poured more troops into Texas and ordered his brother-in-law, General Martin Perfecto de Cós, to take personal command. General Cós promptly ordered the arrest of

Travis and several other Texas troublemakers.

Texians grew fearful. Many of the colonists had been loyal supporters of the Mexican government, but now they turned violently against Santa Anna as they witnessed the arrest of good friends and faced the threat of martial law and military occupation. It appeared that war was unavoidable, and Committees of Safety sprang up in every town to aid in their defense.

After eighteen months in Mexican prisons, Stephen Austin suddenly reappeared in Texas in early September 1835. Although he had preached peace and conciliation for more than a dozen years, Austin was convinced that a peaceful solution was no longer possible. Even as General Cós landed at Copano Bay with a force of 500 Mexican reinforcements bound for the garrison at San Antonio, Austin issued a call to arms. "War," explained Austin, "is our only recourse." He called for volunteers to come forward, organize themselves into companies and mobilize on September 28. Immediately Texians began to volunteer for military companies.

General Cós arrived in San Antonio and went to work searching houses, disarming the Texians and disbanding suspicious groups which reformed as quickly as his troops broke them up. Tension spread throughout the Texas colonies. Shortly afterward, the Mexican garrison at San Antonio received news that the colonists at Gonzales were "shining up a cannon," an old six pounder given them years ago to ward off marauding Indians. The garrison commander sent Lt. Francisco Castaneda with perhaps 100 men to seize the artillery piece. He reached Gonzales on September 29, and found the gun was well hidden. The Texians refused to surrender the cannon, and told Castenada to "come and take it." Two days later the cannon was fired, and the roar was followed by the crack of Kentucky rifles. And so began the Texas Revolution.

The War for Texas Independence lasted less than seven months, consisted of a handful of battles, and was fought by forces numbering less than 10,000 men; probably less than 2,500 ever engaged in a single action. Although these numbers pale in comparison to the wars that came before and those which would follow, the Mexican War was by all accounts an epic struggle of heroic proportions, one which changed the course of Texas and impacted both nations forever.

The most famous engagement of the revolution is the Battle of the Alamo, where some 183 to 250 Texians made their last stand. None were professional soldiers. They came from eighteen states and five European countries. At least 20 were born in Europe, with two recent arrivals from Germany and four from England. They had come to Texas for a multitude of reasons, but they shared a common bond: all were willing to take a stand for liberty.

A fact, by definition, is the quality of being actual. Therein rested the challenge in compiling this book. Separating fact from myth is never easy, and it is particularly difficult when dealing with the events at the Alamo, the greatest story in Texas history. With larger-than-life characters, unlikely heroes, tyranny, oppression, undaunted bravery on both sides, courageous deeds and unwavering sacrifice, it is no wonder that myths abound— it's what legends are made of. And while there is usually some grain of truth at the root of every myth, it should never blind us to reality. The truth is often much richer than any legend.

Facts about the siege and battle of the Alamo are not easy to come by. Problems with dates, names, and places complicate our best efforts. More importantly, little was written down and none of the Texian participants lived to tell the story. No one will ever possess all the facts or know all the answers, but perhaps some of the evidence presented in this book will help to shed some light on some of the more intriguing mysteries.

This book contains a multitude of facts on the mission, the battles, the events and the men who directed their course. My purpose is to entertain, educate, and honor the memories of those men who gave all they had to give so many years ago. Though they died at the Alamo, they live on because we choose to remember. For it is in remembering that we pay them the highest tribute.

May we never forget the Alamo!

Acknowledgements

It's been said many times and in many ways, that no book is the work of one person, and I would like to thank the following people for their help with the preparation of this one.

Jerry Russell of Civil War Round Table Associates, for developing the original concept for the "Facts About" series; my publisher, Theodore P. Savas of Savas Publishing Company, for bringing the idea to fruition and allowing me the opportunity to write this book; Lee W. Merideth, who helped provide direction for this project and whose own book, *1912 Facts About Titanic*, opened this series; Monalisa DiAngelo for her assistance in formatting and interior design; The Daughters of the Republic of Texas History Research Library for allowing me the use of their outstanding collection and for their personal assistance in helping me locate relevant material during my research at San Antonio; and John Anderson, Preservation Officer at Texas State Library and Archives Commission, who was invaluable in locating and obtaining the photographs for this work.

Special thanks to William C. Davis, a source of inspiration for many years, who generously shared his time and insights. Thanks also to Randy Holderfield for his creative and editorial assistance and constant encouragement.

And finally, thanks to my mother, Claudia, and my daughters, Nikki and Shani for their patience, love and support.

Chapter One

Mission San Antonio de Valero
The Alamo

The Mission San Antonio de Valero was the first of a chain of missions to be built along the San Antonio River. It was not until the early 1800s that the mission became known as the Alamo. The following is a brief history of the mission that William Barret Travis would later call the "Key to Texas."

The Mission Period, 1718-1793

■ Father Antonio Olivares founded the Mission San Antonio de Valero in 1718 on the west bank of San Pedro Creek, although its exact location is unknown. The township of San Antonio de Béxar was founded at the same time.

■ The mission was moved to the east side of the San Antonio River after a year on the original site.

■ A hurricane destroyed the mission and the mission moved to its third and final site two blocks to the north.

■ The long barracks, a two-story building, was the first permanent structure on the site. The first floor was five equal size rooms with the stairs located in the center section. The south end contained the living quarters for the priests, the mission's offices, and a dining hall and kitchen.

1744   The cornerstone of the new stone church was laid. This building was destroyed in a storm and construction began on a replacement. An adobe hall was used as a temporary church. Four bells were mounted on a forked post in front.

1758   The present church was started and the date (1758), was inscribed across the door. The church was never fully completed.

1767   The exterior of the church was finished and Dionicio de Jesús Gonzales was hired to carve the ornamental entrance to Mission San Antonio de Valero. Gonzales was paid 1,500 pesos for his work.

1790   The Indian population of the mission dropped from a high of 300 to only forty-eight. Many died from disease (an epidemic in 1739 killed 116 Indians). Indian tribes living at the Alamo during the mission's early years included members of the Lipan Apahces, Sanas, Scipxames, Tamiques, Tops, Cocos, Jaranames, Pataguas, Payayas, Yierbipiames, Yutas, and Kiowas.

1793   The Mission San Antonio de Valero was closed down by order of the Spanish government (as were all the missions in the area). Its lands were distributed among the remaining thirty-nine mission Indians.

The Alamo (1793 - 1835)

1793   The mission became known as Pueblo of Valero. It was a self-governing town separate from San Antonio de Béxar across the river.

1801   A Spanish Cavalry unit stationed in Mexico was sent to occupy the old mission. The "Second Flying Company of San Carlos de Parras" came from the pueblo in Mexico, El Alamo de Parras. Most historians believe the name Alamo was given to the compound because of the soldiers from el Alamo, Mexico.

1805   The Alamo was the site of the first hospital in Texas. On October 19, 1805, Col. Don Antonio Cordero, Governor of Coahuila, Texas and commander of the frontier, wrote to his commanding general, Brig. Gen. Nemerio Salcedo: "I have provided, without any cost whatever, and availing myself only of a little arbitration, the equipment of a partly ruined chamber in a secularized Mission de Valero as a military infirmary. I have had it provided with beds made of reeds in order to avoid the dampness of the ground. The patients of all the companies or posts who may be sent here will be placed in them under the necessary care of a nurse (male), a woman to take care of the kitchen and guard of the company of the Alamo which is stationed at this mission. The only expenses entailed will be the increase of the troops one real and a half per day to two reales, and the remuneration of the doctor and cost of medicines."

During the Mexican War for Independence (1810-1821), the Alamo was the site of much activity and changed hands several times between Spanish royalists and rebels.

1821-   The Alamo was under Mexican occupation.
1835

1827   Anastacio Bustamente, a future president of Mexico, deserves recognition as the first savior of the Alamo. The state legislature had considered tearing down the mission and selling the rock in the walls for cash at public auction, as they were in desperate need of money. Bustamente wanted the old buildings to be permanently used as barracks for the Alamo company and demanded that the fort be spared.

The Alamo 1835-1836

■ The church building in 1835 lacked the distinctive "hump" and upper row of windows that we see today. These were added, along with a roof, when the U.S. Army took over the site during the Mexican-American war.

■ The precise dimensions and plan of the Alamo in 1835-1836 are not known with any certainty. No two plans or sketches of the place from contemporary sources are in more than general agreement.

■ The Alamo, like the four other missions along the San Antonio, was constructed in the Franciscan pattern. The majority of the fortification was made of adobe and unquarried limestone, with walls two to three feet thick and nine to twelve feet high.

■ The heart of the compound was a rough rectangle of bare ground known as the "plaza." This plaza covered about three acres and was bordered by walls and buildings. On the south side was a long one-story building called the "low barracks," which was divided by the main entrance into the court, a 10-foot wide porte-cochere. A line of adobe huts, linked and protected by a stone wall about 12 feet high ran along the west side. Another stone wall ran along the north side of the plaza. The east side was banked by the so-called "long barracks." This two-story building was almost 200 feet long and was very strong and received extra protection from walls bordering a corral behind it.

■ The thirty-foot high chapel was the Alamo's highest point and the sturdiest building in the compound. The cut stone and mortar walls were four feet thick and twenty-two feet high. There were several small rooms along the side, which were arched and well covered.

■ The church was set back so far that it didn't meet the south side of the compound. This created a gap of about fifty yards. During the Texian occupation, chief engineer Green Jamison built a palisade of sticks and dirt to close this gap.

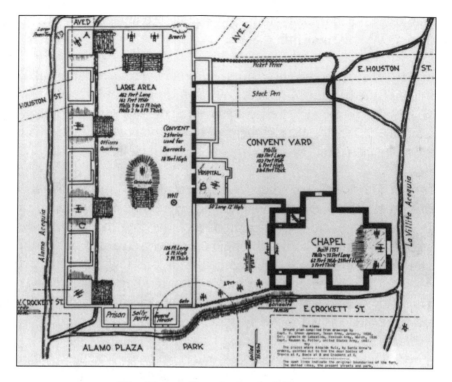

The Alamo. Site plan by A. J. Houston.

Ground plan compiled from drawings by Captain B. Green Jameson, Texas Army, January, 1836, Colonel Ignacio de Labastida, Mexican Army, March 1836, Captain Reuben M. Potter, United States Army, 1841.

Key: The places where Alcade Ruiz, by Santa Anna's orders, pointed out to him the dead bodies of Travis at A, Bowie at B, and Crockett at C.

The open lines indicate the original boundaries of the fort; the dotted lines, the present streets and park; and the heavy lines, the boundaries of the State property.
Texas State Library & Archives Commission

Fortifying the Alamo; October 1835 – March 1836

■ The Alamo played a central role in the Texas War for Independence. It was the site of two sieges and changed hands three times during the war. General Cós arrived in San Antonio with 500 Mexican soldiers on October 11, 1835 to counter a rebellion that had just resulted in a shootout at Gonzales. He immediately put his men to work fortifying the Alamo.

■   The Alamo was not built as a military garrison and it lacked many of the basic requirements of a fort. For example: there were no bastions protecting exterior walls, terraces were scarce or nonexistent along some walls, and there were few gunports through which the riflemen or artillery could fire on the enemy in relative safety.

■   The Mexican soldiers under General Cós constructed most of the defenses of the Alamo. Trenches were dug, dirt was piled up in ramps and platforms for cannons to shoot over the walls, and a stockade was built across the open cemetery area in front of the church. The roof over the church had been torn down for defensive reasons. The rubble from the roof was packed against the eastern wall and covered with earth to form the ramp leading up to the 12-pounder cannon sited above the apse.

■   After the Alamo was back in Texian hands, engineer Green Jamison threw up platforms of earth and timber along the walls to serve as parapets and gun mounts. By February 1836, 18 to 21 guns had been mounted, mostly along the walls, but with two mounted in the interior facing the main gate.

■   The Alamo's 18-pounder was the biggest gun in Texas. It was placed in the southwest angle, where it commanded the town. The 18-pounder could throw a solid iron ball more than half a mile beyond the western outskirts of the town.

■   The north wall of the Alamo was weak. It was in ruins before the Texians laid siege to the Alamo in November 1835. The Texians packed dirt against the wall to strengthen it. The act did more harm than good, since they now had no walkway along the interior wall and were forced to stand up on it in order to fire with their guns--making themselves perfect targets in the process.

■ Field works were erected inside the enclosure, and the interior walls of many of the buildings were pierced to provide passage from room to room if the main plaza was lost to the enemy.

■ In order to prevent the enemy from cutting off the water supply that ran through the plaza, the Texians opened an old well.

Aftermath (May 1836)

■ The Mexicans left the Alamo in ruins. General Andrade received orders dated May 19, 1836 to spike all the cannon and throw the ammunition in the river, destroy all small arms, and demolish the fortifications at the Alamo. Andrade and his troops left on May 24.

■ Dr. J. H Bernard was an eyewitness to the destruction of the Alamo. He wrote in his journal: "Tuesday, May 24, 1836. As soon as the troops left town this morning, a large fire streamed up from the Alamo. . . .We found the fire proceeding from a church where a platform had been built extending from the great door to the top wall on the back side. . . .This was made of wood and was too far consumed. . .to extinguish it. . . .The Alamo was completely dismantled, all single walls were leveled, the fosse filled up, and the pickets torn up and burnt."

The Alamo (1849 to the present)

■ The United States rented the Alamo in 1849, restored the chapel and added the rounded top on the existing facade.

■ The Alamo was surrendered to the Confederacy in 1861, but at the end of the Civil War was returned to the United States, which continued to rent it as a depot until 1876.

1877   Honore Grenet bought the long barrack building and court-yard on the north side of the Alamo for $20,000. His remodeling included a two-story porch on the west and south side, three wooden towers with wooden fake cannons and an enclosed courtyard on the east. He had a museum and a grocery store that also sold wine and liquor. The store was sold to Hugo and Schmeltzer Company for $28,000 in 1886.

1883   The old Alamo church was sold to the Sate of Texas for $20,000 on May 16, 1883, the first step in historical preservation.

■   A hotel syndicate offered to buy the Alamo and build a hotel in 1903. The Daughters of the Republic of Texas, who had already been working to save the old missions, began efforts to raise the $75,000 they needed to purchase the property. Adina de Zavala, of the de Zavala Chapter, convinced Clara Driscoll, a lady of wealth, to assist them. Clara Driscoll provided about $65,000 when private donations amounted to less than $10,000. Governor S. W. T. Lanham signed legislation on January 26, 1905, for state funding to reimburse Driscoll. On October 4, 1905, the church and long barrack was conveyed to the Daughters of the Republic of Texas.

■   The Alamo has been administered and maintained by the Daughters of the Republic of Texas without charge to the state since 1905.

■   The long barracks was restored in 1968 and opened to the public as a museum.

Chapter Two

Chronology of the Texas War for Independence

The following is a chronology of the major events of the Texas War for Independence.

Sept. 29, 1835: Lieutenant Francisco Castañeda arrives at Gonzales and demands the return of the cannon from the colonists.

Oct. 2, 1835 Battle of Gonzales (Mexican troops withdraw).

Oct. 9, 1835: Battle of Goliad (Mexican troops surrender).

Oct. 11, 1835: Stephen Austin elected commander of the "Volunteer Army of the People."

Oct. 28, 1835: Battle of Concepción (Mexican troops with draw).

Nov. 1, 1835: Austin begins 34-day siege of San Antonio.

Nov. 3, 1835: Texians capture Fort Lipantitlan.

Nov. 3-14, 1835: Consultation meets in San Felipe for the purpose of establishing a provisional government. Austin appointed commissioner to U.S. and Sam

	Houston appointed commander-in-chief of the Regular army.
Nov. 4, 1835:	Battle of Nueces Crossing (Mexican troops withdraw.)
Nov. 26, 1835:	The Grass Fight (Mexican troops withdraw).
Dec. 5-9, 1835:	Battle of Béxar (San Antonio). General Martin Perfecto de Cós surrenders.
Jan. 19, 1836:	Colonel James Bowie and his contingent ride into the Alamo.
Feb. 3, 1836:	Lieutenant Colonel William Barret Travis and his thirty troopers arrive at the Alamo.
Feb. 8, 1836:	David Crockett arrives at the Alamo with the Tennessee Mounted Volunteers.
Feb. 11, 1836:	Travis named commander of the Alamo.
Feb. 11-26, 1836:	Travis and Bowie share joint command of the Alamo.
Feb. 23, 1836:	General Antonio Lopez de Santa Anna begins 12-day siege of the Alamo.
Feb. 24, 1836:	Travis writes letter to "The People of Texas & all Americans in the world."
Feb. 24, 1836:	Bowie is incapacitated due to illness; Travis takes full command.
Feb. 27, 1836:	Battle of San Patricio (Mexican victory).
Mar. 1, 1836:	The "Gonzales 32" arrive at the Alamo. They are the only relief force to come to the aid of the Alamo garrison.

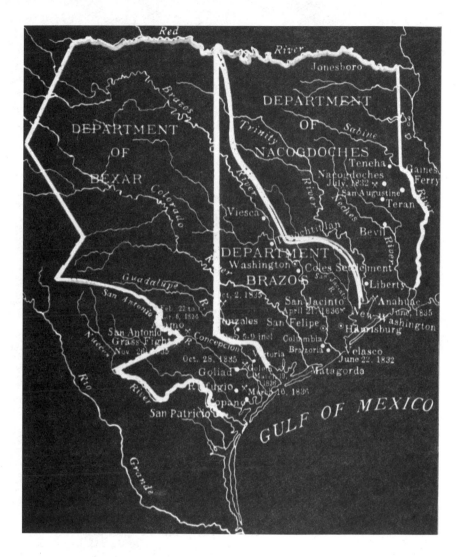

Texas in 1835. This map shows the boundaries of the Departments of Brazos, Béxar, and Nachogdoches, as they existed in 1835. The location and dates of the battles for Texas Independence are also listed. *Texas State Library & Archves Commission*

Mar. 2, 1836:   The Convention at Washington-on-the-Brazos votes unanimously for a declaration of independence.

Mar. 2, 1836:   Battle of Agua Dulce (Mexican victory).

Mar. 4, 1836:   The Convention appoints Houston commander-in-chief of the Army of the Republic of Texas.

Mar. 6, 1836:   The Fall of the Alamo.

Mar. 12-14, 1836: Battle of Refugio. Captain Amon B. King and Colonel William Ward run short of ammunition and attempt to escape rather than surrender.

Mar. 15, 1836:   Colonel King's men captured near Refugio.

Mar. 16, 1836:   King's men taken to Refugio and executed.

Mar. 18, 1836:   Cavalry skirmish at Goliad.

Mar. 19-20, 1836: Battle of Coleto. Colonel James Fannin surrenders. Fannin's men marched back to Goliad under guard.

Mar. 21, 1836:   Battle of Copano. Colonel Ward surrenders. Ward's men march back to Goliad where they are held with Fannin's command.

Mar. 27, 1836:   Palm Sunday. Three hundred and forty-two prisoners are marched out of Goliad and executed.

Apr. 7, 1836:   Santa Anna attacks Captain Moseley Baker, Houston's rear guard, at San Felipe Ford.

Apr. 12, 1836:   Santa Anna outflanks Captain Baker. Baker retreats.

Apr. 20-21, 1836: Battle of San Jacinto. A Texian victory and final battle of the Texas War for Independence.

Apr. 22, 1836:   Santa Anna is captured and taken prisoner.

Chapter Three

The Texian Army

The Army of the People

The Texian army began with a group of colonists determined to defend their country and their rights. New recruits poured into Gonzales after they received news of the first Texian victory at Gonzales on October 2, 1835. According to one of these recruits, Noah Smithwick, "Some were for independence, some were for the Constitution of 1824, and some were for anything, just so long as it was a row."

■ On October 11, 1835, Stephen Austin was elected commander of the "Volunteer Army of the People." The army consisted of only some three hundred soldiers.

■ Volunteers were the rank and file of the Texian army. Only a small number of them had lived in Texas for more than a few months or years. Almost all of the men who lost their lives at the Alamo and at Goliad were newly arrived volunteers from the United States.

■ Tejano volunteers made up about 5% of the force. Juan Seguín formed a company of Tejano ranchers and performed invaluable work for Houston, Travis, and Bowie.

■ The promise of free land helped swell enlistments. Volunteers were promised land in exchange for military service in the rebel army: 1280 acres for those who remained in service until the end of the fighting, 640 acres for six months' service, and 320 acres for three months.

■ Appeals for volunteers appeared in newspapers all over the states. A letter written by Sam Houston in October 1835 appeared in the Natchitoches, Louisiana *Red River Herald:* "Let each man come with a good rifle and 100 rounds of ammunition—and come soon."

■ The New Orleans "Greys," named for the color of their uniforms, were some of the first men to answer the Texas call for volunteers. The Mobile Greys were close behind and reached San Antonio on December 12.

■ There were no provisions for the army. Each soldier supplied his own weapon and horse or mule. There were also no uniforms. According to volunteer Noah Smithwick, "the nearest approach [to a uniform was] buckskin breeches, with wide diversity even there, some being new and soft and yellow, while others, from long familiarity with rain and grease and dirt, had become hard and black, and shiny."

The Army of the Republic of Texas

■ The Texians established a provisional government in November 1835. One of their first acts was to authorize the creation of an army, which was to be commanded by Sam Houston as major general and commander-in-chief under the authority of Governor Henry Smith.

■ The new army was to consist of 1,120 men plus some headquarters personnel and regimental staffs. Half of the army would be composed of Regulars enlisted for two years and half of volunteers enlisted for the duration of the war. The army was to include a small general staff, one regular and two volunteer regiments of infantry, and a regular regiment of artillery. Provision was made for the raising of a paramilitary force of 150 Rangers. The delegates later authorized the creation of a Cavalry Corps of 384 men. This brought the authorized strength of the army, with the Rangers, to about 1,700 men (including staffs).

■ Militia units were to be organized on a local basis with a provision for election of officers. All able-bodied men in Texas between the ages of 16 and 50 were liable for militia service.

■ An "Auxiliary Corps of Volunteers" and a "Reserve Army" were also authorized under the provisional government for the enlistment of additional troops. The reserve army was never activated and didn't enroll a single man before the end of the war.

■ The Texas Rangers were formally organized in 1835, although they had been in existence for many years prior. During the revolution, these companies served as scouts, reconnaissance "spies," and as a rear guard to round up citizen stragglers during the "Runaway Scrape."

■ The Texas Rangers (150 men) were required to furnish their own horses and weapons for a daily pay of $1.25. They shunned uniforms and lived mostly on wild game while on the trail.

Organization

■ The regulations of the United States Army were adopted for use in so far as they suited the needs of Texas.

■ The staff of the army was to consist of the commander-in-chief plus an adjutant general, an inspector general, and four aides-de-camp.

■ Regiments of infantry, whether regular, volunteer, auxiliary or militia, were to consist of five companies of 56 men each, with a staff of four.

■ The Cavalry Corps, commanded by Lieutenant Colonel William B. Travis, was to consist of six companies of 64 troopers each, plus a staff of three or four. The corps did not play much of a role in the war, since Travis was only able to recruit about 30 men.

Chapter Four

The Mexican Army

The "Army of Operations" was about four times larger than the U.S. Army but had 33 times more generals. Recruiting was a political affair and resulted in many officers who were unsuited for command responsibilities. At the beginning of the Texas campaign, some sources estimate the number of men and officers at 6,000-6,100.

Mexican Order of Battle in Texas

■   Although changes in the order of battle occurred throughout the campaign, in December 1835 the Army of Operations for Texas was organized as follows:

■   1st Division (or Vanguard Brigade)
   General Joaquin Ramirez y Sesma
   Matamoros Battalion
   Jiménez Battalion
   San Luis Potosi Battalion
   Dolores Cavalry
   62 artillerymen

■   2nd Division
   General Antonio López de Santa Anna

■ 1st Brigade
General Antonio Gaona
Aldama Battalion
Toluca Battalion
Queretaro Battalion
San Luis Potosi Battalion (detachment)
Guanajuato
63 artillerymen

■ 2nd Brigade
General Eugenio Tolsa
Guerrero Battalion
Mexico City Battalion
Guadalajara Battalion
60 artillerymen

■ Cavalry
General Juan José de Andrade
Tampico Regiment
Cuautla Regiment
Guanajuato Regiment
San Luis Potosi Regiment
Bajio Regiment

■ Zapadores
Lt. Col. Augustin Amat
185 men

■ The force besieging the Alamo comprised the Matamoros, San Luis Potosi, Aldama, Toluca and Jiménez Battalions; Zapadores, and some cavalry and artillery under General Sesma.

Organization

■ The Mexican army consisted of several contingents. Regular forces, or *permanentes*, the garrison troops or *presidiales* and *auxiliares*, and the semi-regular state troops, or *activos*.

■ *Permanentes* were the regular forces supported by the central government. The *presidiales* and *auxiliares* were usually stationed at frontier outposts and were often busy dealing with the Indians, which probably made them the best troops in the Mexican army. *Activos* were frequently used for service during rebellions, and some of these soldiers were fairly professional.

■ The Mexican army reorganized their battalions in December 1835. The ten regular battalions of infantry were renamed for heroes of the War of Independence from Spain:

Hidalgo	Landero
Allende	Matamoros
Morelos	Jiménez
Guerrero	Abasolo
Aldama	Galeana

■ The six regular cavalry regiments were named after battlefields of the revolution:

Dolores	Cuautla
Iguala	Veracruz
Palamar	Tampico

■ The organization of all three components was essentially the same. Infantry regiments normally consisted of one battalion, which comprised eight companies. Each company was supposed to have 120 men. With a staff of 25, total battalion strength was 985 officers and men. Casualties, disease, and desertion guaranteed that a regiment was never at full strength. Companies usually had from 35 to 65 men, with battalions running about 275 to 500 men.

■ Two companies of each battalion were "elite" companies, one of *granaderos* or heavy infantry, and one of *cazadores* or light infantry. The *granaderos* were traditionally recruited from the biggest and bravest in the regiment, while the *cazadores* were drawn from the smallest of the bravest men. In battle, the elite companies were normally deployed on the extreme right or left of their regiments and were sometimes known as "flank" companies.

■ *Zapadores*, the engineering troops, were the elite regiment of the Mexican army. They were organized and most often served as an infantry battalion. There were only 185 men in this regiment.

■ Cavalry regiments consisted of four squadrons. Each squadron had a staff of three, plus two troops of seventy-one mounted and eight dismounted men each, for a total of 161 officers and men. A regiment with four full squadrons plus its staff of 20 and service detachment of fourteen technicians ran to 678 officers and men. However, regiments normally ran to 200-300 men with squadrons often of no more than fifty to seventy-five men.

Manpower

■ Soldiers were either volunteers on eight-year enlistments or conscripts serving ten years. Volunteers were few, and the army was forced to turn to conscription. As a result, many recruits were liberated convicts. The draft, known as *sorteo*, was simply a drawing of lots. However, one source called the lottery a mass kidnapping. "Here are 300 volunteers," wrote a recruiting officer to a senior officer. "I will send you 300 more if you return the chains."

■ The average Mexican soldier was between 5' and 5'6" in height (each was measured to a sixteenth of an inch). At 5'10", Santa Anna was one of the tallest soldiers in the Mexican army.

Training

■ Training of the troops was almost nonexistent. The Mexican army was supposed to be trained to use flexible tactics combining infantry, cavalry, and artillery. In practice, however, the training was so rudimentary that the only tactic most knew was the frontal attack, with the men firing their muskets from the hip as they advanced, and then closing with the bayonet.

Uniforms

■ Officers' uniforms were styled after Napoleon and his troops. In fact, their dress uniforms were often discards or surplus items from various Napoleonic armies. Mexican officers wore dark blue uniforms with gold epaulets. Dragoons (horse soldiers) were even more picturesque with their polished helmets and lances.

■ The Mexican soldiers wore tall black leather shakos for their heads and many wore work clothes made out of white cotton or linen clothing (completely unsuitable for Texas winters). By the time the Mexican soldiers reached the Alamo, their shoes and sandals had given out and their shirts had rotted. They looked more like refugees than soldiers.

Equipment and Provisions

■ Soldiers were issued a knapsack, a pair of shoes, a pair of extra sandals, two changes of clothing, a cape, a canteen, a plate, one round of cartridges, one flint and one gun.

■ Food was provided to soldiers below the rank of first sergeant. This food allotment consisted of only half rations: one pound of meat and some beans or corn per day. The soldiers ate only eight ounces of toasted corn cake daily for the last 30 days before reaching San Antonio.

■ Officers were forced to use their wages to purchase supplies. The idea that they had to pay for their own food outraged and demoralized them. As a result, they had to pay sky-high prices to feed not only themselves but their families as well (many of whom trailed along behind the army). When supplies ran low, they bribed the quartermasters, and dipped into their troops' rations when money ran out.

■ Mexican soldiers were paid 20 pesos 8/23 granos per a twenty-five-day month.

The Long March North

■ The Yucatan Battalion was almost entirely composed of men recently recruited in tropical Yucatan. The troops suffered from the unusually cold weather which plagued the army during the march north into Texas. In his diary, Brig. Gen. Jose Urrea recorded the deaths from exposure of six men from the Yucatan Battalion within hours of the onset of the "Blue Norther" of February 25.

■ The camp follower was a permanent fixture of the nine-teenth-century Mexican army. *Soladeras* (soldier's women) made good cooks, foragers and nurses. Many in the army were concerned about their presence. They consumed needed supplies, slowed the line of march, and proved a distraction to the husband-soldiers who cared more about their families than their duty. However, it was widely accepted that if the women went home, so would the soldiers.

■ The Mexican army boasted a medical corps, but in his haste to get the expedition to Texas underway, Santa Anna neglected to make provisions for proper medical care on the march. The only physician that accompanied the army part of the way turned out to be a fraud. There were no beds, no medicine, no utensils, and no surgical equipment with the army. As a result, many soldiers died along the way from food poisoning, hypothermia, and contaminated drinking water.

■ In the whole Catholic Mexican army, there was not a single priest.

Chapter Five

Tejano Revolutionaries

Many of the local Tejanos supported the Texas Revolution and some were even eager to serve in the Texian ranks. Juan Seguín and his company of vaquero scouts made the Texian Revolution their revolution. Lorenzo de Zavala, the Mexican politician, sat at the Texas Constitutional Convention with two other Mexicans. Risking everything, these men were forced to betray their country of birth in the pursuit of liberty.

■ General Stephen Austin recognized the value of Tejano equestrian skills and appointed Juan Seguín a captain of cavalry. He was authorized to raise a company of *vaqueros,* which would provide "essential service" as mounted troopers. According to William T. Austin, Gen. Austin's aide, "These mexicans being well acquainted with the country, were of important service as express riders, guides to foraging parties, &c." The Tejanos brought critically needed range skills to the Texian army.

■ The contributions of federalist Tejanos were crucial to the campaign to capture Fort Lipantitlan in October 1835. The security of Goliad required the Texians to take Lipantitlan before it was reinforced by 400 to 500 horsemen reportedly on their way to strengthen the post. Captain Philip Dimitt, Goliad's commander, sent a detachment of thirty-five men to reduce and burn the Mexican garrison. The expedition could not have left Goliad if Tejanos had not provided food and horses. The *rancheros* of Goliad furnished twenty horses for the expedition, and those of Guadalupe Victoria donated thirty head of cattle.

■ There were at least sixty-seven Tejanos who joined the Texians during the Battle of Béxar (San Antonio) in December 1835. The Mexican cavalrymen, who were not used to fighting on foot, tethered their horses and joined their Texian comrades as infantrymen.

■ Captain Placido Benavides, mayor of Victoria, organized a company of thirty ranchers and joined the Texian forces at Victoria on October 7, 1835. These men fought under Capt. George Collinsworth at Goliad and reinforced the Texian army at the Battle of Béxar, on December 5-9, 1835.

■ José Cassiano, a San Antonio merchant, served as a scout along the Rio Grande to gather information on Santa Anna's troop movements. If that weren't enough, he gave the Texian army the use of his home and store, with all its supplies.

■ José Antonio Navarro was a Texas patriot and one of four delegates from San Antonio to the Convention of 1836. He and his uncle were the only native-born Texians to sign the Declaration of Independence. Navarro was imprisoned for three and one-half years in a Mexican dungeon for his participation in the Santa Fe Expedition of 1841. He was under constant pressure to foreswear his allegiance to Texas, but refused to do so. "I have sworn to be a good Texan, and that I will not foreswear. I will die for that which I firmly believe, for I know it is just and right. One life is a small price for a cause so great. As I fought, so shall I be willing to die. I will never forsake Texas and her cause. I am her son."

■ Lorenzo de Zavala was an ardent Federalist and an important Mexican political figure while still in his mid-20s. Zavala was a member of the assembly of 1823-1824, which drew up the liberal Federal Constitution of 1824. He was elected to the first Senate in 1824 and governor of the State of Mexico in 1827. He resigned the latter post to become Minister of Finance. As Santa Anna moved to a centralist position, Zavala broke with him, traveled to Texas in

Juan Nepomuceno Seguín. He made the Texian Revolution his revolution, but why was a true hero in the fight for Texas Independence forced to flee to Mexico?
Texas State Library & Archives Commission

1835, and became one of the most active revolutionary leaders. Zavala took part in the "Consultation" of October-November 1835 and was a signer of the Texas Declaration of Independence. He served as the first vice-president of the Republic of Texas.

■ As commander of the Alamo garrison, Travis used Captain Seguín's men to maintain a constant stream of patrols and scouts to monitor the roads leading to the Rio Grande.

■ The Tejano scouts generally brought accurate intelligence often at great risk to themselves. On February 20, Juan Seguín's scouts reported Santa Anna's vanguard had crossed the Rio Grande. Texian leaders discussed the possibility, but there had been so many rumors of Santa Anna's approach that some refused to believe it. Some of the Texians put little faith in reports of Tejanos, since many were known to be *centralistas*. In any event, it appears no action was taken. Unfortunately for the Texians, these reports were correct; Santa Anna had indeed crossed the Rio Grande.

■ Following the fall of the Alamo, Colonel Juan Seguín led a detachment of nineteen men at San Jacinto despite the fact they had been excused from duty (Houston feared that they might be mistaken for the enemy in the heat of battle). Seguín reminded Houston that he had also lost men at the Alamo. Furthermore, his men were all from the San Antonio area and could not go home until Santa Anna had been driven out of Texas. Seguín asserted that his men had more reason to hate *santanistas* than anyone in Texas did, and they wanted in on the kill. "Spoken like a man!" Houston responded. But Houston had one condition: Seguín and his men had to place a piece of cardboard in their hatbands to identify them. With cardboard insignia in place, Seguín and his brave soldiers advanced with the rest of the Texian army.

■ Mexican soldiers sought mercy from Seguín's men at San Jacinto. A Mexican officer recognized Antonio Menchaca as an acquaintance from San Antonio and pleaded with him as a "brother Mexican" to intercede for his life. Menchaca replied, "No damn you, I'm no Mexican—I'm an American." Then turning to his Anglo comrades, he instructed, "Shoot him!"

■ Several Tejanos in Seguín's company made claims against the Republic of Texas for service during the revolution. Their claims indicated that they had entered the service at varying times but all listed their termination date as February 20 and 21, 1836. Their claims went unpaid. However, they should not be judged too harshly. When Seguín learned that Santa Anna's vanguard had crossed the Rio Grande, he requested furlough for some of his men whose families and farms lay in the path of the Mexican advance. These men left with Travis' permission. They left for the same reason many Texians did during the "Runaway Scrape"—to provide for the safety of their families.

The Tide Turns

■ Many Tejanos who fought so courageously with their Texian comrades found bitterness and resentment after the revolution. Juan Seguín fought in almost every campaign of the Texas Revolution and buried the remains of the Alamo defenders, many of whom were his friends. He was elected mayor of San Antonio in 1840. Forced to resign from office two years later, he fled to Mexico with his family fearing for his safety. Many Tejanos who had supported the independence movement in Texas shared the fate of Seguín. Original American settlers got along well with them, but those who came later treated them with hostility and abuse.

Juan Seguín and his men

■ The following is a list of some of Juan Seguín's men who served in the Texas struggle for independence:

Juan Abamillo	Domingo Días	José María Guerrero
Juan Antonio Badillo	Francisco Díaz	Antonio Hernández
Andrés Barcinas	Gregorio Esparza	Gregorio Hernández
Clemente Bustillos	Manuel Flores	Toribio Losoya
Luis Castañón	Antonio Fuentes	Pablo Mansola
Agapito Cervantes	Clemente García	Antonio Menchaca
Carlos Chacón	Jesús Garcia	Andrés Nava
Antonio Cruz y Arocha	Alejandro de la Garza	Anselmo Vergara

Chapter Six

The Revolution at Sea

The importance of the naval aspects of the Texas War for Independence is often overlooked, even though it was through command of the sea lanes that Texas' independence was assured. At the time of the revolution, the most efficient way of getting to Texas, whether from Mexico or the United States, was by water. The journey through the Gulf of Mexico to Anahuac or Brazoria, or any of the other inlets and bays, was easier, cheaper, and healthier. The overland route from Mexico ran across seemingly endless semi-desert terrain, while the trip from the United States was partially across somewhat less extensive malarial marshlands and partially across flat prairies. Most of the American settlers arrived by sea.

■ There were eight naval actions between September 1, 1835 and April 3, 1836.

■ The first maritime engagement of the revolution took place off Velasco on September 1, 1835. The Mexican armed transport *Correo de Mejico* seized an American-owned merchantman with improper papers. A band of heavily armed Texians put out to sea on the small unarmed steamer *Laura* to retake the ship. The Texians liberated the merchant vessel after *Correo de Mejico* became becalmed.

■ A more important naval action took place on September 2, 1835. The jointly owned American-Texan armed schooner *San Felipe* turned up off Velasco bearing a special cargo: Stephen Austin and a load of arms. Austin was returning from Mexico to deliver the call to arms against Mexican centralism. *Laura* sortied out to tow *San Felipe* into port. The skipper of *Correo de Mejico* maneuvered his ship and brought *San Felipe* under fire. *San Felipe* returned fire while still under tow. After Austin disembarked, *San Felipe* was towed back out to sea so that she could engage the Mexican vessel. The fight went on much of the day, but *Correjo de Mejico* had the worst of it and struck her colors the following morning.

■ Mexico controlled the seas during the early months of the revolution. The armed schooners *Montezuma* and *Veracruzana* were in Texas waters escorting supply and troop ships throughout October and November of 1835.

■ The purchase of warships ("two schooners of twelve guns each and two schooners of six") was authorized by the provisional government of Texas in November 1835. The government also approved the issuance of letters of marque and reprisal, piracy licenses frequently issued by inferior naval powers, a practice continued well into the nineteenth century. Within weeks, Texas privateers were wrecking havoc with Mexican merchant shipping. Although there were never more than six of these licensed pirates, they seriously interfered with Mexican communications.

■ *William S. Robbins* was the first publicly owned vessel, and thus officially the first ship of the Texas Navy. The armed schooner, under the command of Captain Hurd, was purchased by the Committee of Safety at Matagorda in late November to be used for local defense. The Committee applied for and received a letter of marque on December 5, 1835.

■ An American schooner, *Hannah Alexander*, inbound with arms for Texas forces was intercepted and run aground off Paso Caballo by the Mexican *Bravo* in mid-December, 1835. In her only action conducted under the letter of marque, *William S. Robbins* set sail for Paso Caballo. Captain Hurd retook *Hannah Alexander* without a shot on December 19, 1835.

■ By mid-January of 1836, agents for the provisional Texan government had picked up a former U.S. Revenue Cutter, which was commissioned as *Independence,* as well as the armed schooner *Brutus.* Two privateers, *William S. Robbins* (renamed *Liberty*) and the *Invincible* were also purchased and put out to sea under a pair of brothers, Captain W. S. Brown and Jeremiah Brown, both veteran merchant skippers.

■ On her first voyage, January 10-March 1, 1836, *Independence* operated all the way down to Tampico and captured numerous small Mexican vessels, a cruise which earned her skipper a promotion to commodore.

■ The *Liberty* found the large unarmed Mexican merchantman *Pelicano* lying off Sisal. On the night of March 3, 1836, Captain Brown sent two long boats full of men to capture the ship. The Mexican garrison commander realized what was happening and re-inforced the ship with twenty men. The cutting-out party was forced to wage a brisk fight before it secured control of the ship.

■ *Liberty* captured a fine prize on March 25, 1836. While patrolling in the Gulf of Mexico, she encountered the American-owned brig *Durango,* which was operating under charter to the Mexican army and laden with military supplies.

■ Two Mexican men-of-war, *Bravo* and *General Urrea,* turned up off the port at Matagorda Bay towards the end of March. They had a brief encounter with the *Independence,* which soon withdrew. The Mexican vessels stood out to sea but did not return to port. Commander Hawkins soon discovered the reason for their presence: General José Urrea was advancing up the coast towards Matagorda Bay, and the Mexican ships were escorting a supply ship for General Urrea's benefit. Hawkins withdrew the small Texan fleet to Galveston.

■ The *Invincible* was dispatched to patrol off the mouth of the Rio Grande with the intention of interfering in the movement of Mexican supply ships. On April 3, 1836, she encountered *Bravo* sailing into the Gulf escorting the merchant ship *Correo Segundo*. *Bravo* damaged her rudder crossing the bar at the mouth of the river and was unable to steer. A battle ensued which lasted about an hour, although neither vessel incurred much damage. *Invincible* left the rudderless *Bravo* to pursue a large brig that appeared on the horizon. The ship was *Pocket*, an American merchantman under charter to the Mexican government. She was loaded with military supplies, a number of Mexican naval officers, and a valuable map of the Texas coast.

■ The war at sea came to an end with the capture of Santa Anna at San Jacinto, at least for a time. Although the Texians had not won complete command of the seas off their shore, they had secured their lines of communication with the United States and interfered with those of the Mexican army.

■ In 1845, the Texas Navy was incorporated into the United States Navy.

Warships of the Texas War for Independence

TEXAS

Brutus	schooner
Independence	schooner
Invincible	schooner
Laura	schooner
Liberty	schooner *(ex-William S. Robbins)*
San Felipe	brig

MEXICO

Bravo	schooner *(ex-Montezuma)*
Correo de Mejico	schooner
Correo Segundo	schooner
General Urrea	brig
Veracruzana	schooner

This list does not include any Mexican vessels which were not involved in operations off the coast of Texas, 1835-1836.

Chapter Seven

Grapeshot, Musketshot and the Bayonet

The weapons used in the Texas Revolution were mostly smooth-bore muskets and light artillery. They were similar to the weapons used in the Napoleonic Wars and in some cases had actually been used in those conflicts. While Mexican troops relied heavily on the Brown Bess Musket and the British Baker rifle, the Texian forces began the war with a variety of weapons. Initially, many of them were armed only with shotguns and fowling pieces. By the end of the war, most were equipped with captured Mexican weapons.

Artillery played a relatively minor role in the revolution as a whole, and this was true even at the Alamo. There were less than 50 pieces in use during the entire war, and numerous types were used. The Mexicans had Spanish and French guns, while the Texians had a few pieces, most of which were American-made.

Alamo Firepower

■ The Alamo had been built as a mission and had never been converted to a proper fortress. Green Jamison, the chief engineer, went to work fortifying the Alamo once it was in Texian hands. He threw up platforms of earth and timber along the walls to serve as parapets and gun mounts. By February 1836, 18 to 21 guns had been mounted, mostly along the walls, but two were mounted in the interior facing the main gate.

■ The Alamo's 18-pound artillery piece was the biggest gun in Texas. It was placed in the southwest angle were it commanded the town. The 18-pounder could throw a solid iron ball more than half a mile beyond the western outskirts of the town.

■ One of the Alamo guns was a "gunade," a short-range naval gun of the period. It has not been determined why a ship's gunade had been taken to a post 150 miles from the nearest coast. Engineer Green Jamison reportedly mounted the naval ordnance piece on the west wall.

■ During the first week of the siege, solid balls blew the plaza to pieces. According to William C. Davis, author of *Three Roads to the Alamo*, some two hundred shots had rained down into the Alamo, but no one had been killed or injured. Fortunately many of the Mexican guns were of the same caliber as the garrison's guns, and the solid shot was picked up and fired back. By nightfall on March 5, the Mexicans had fired about 334 solid shot at the walls, and another 86 rounds of exploding shells. The garrison was falling apart faster than its occupants could repair it.

■ Most of the initial Mexican casualties were caused by grapeshot (smaller iron balls used mainly as an anti-personnel weapon). It could have been worse. Unfortunately for the defenders, there were not enough men to man all of the Alamo's 18 cannon (which would have required 90 men) and man the walls.

■ The Alamo powder magazine was located in the baptistery, a room to the right of the main church door. Its south wall formed part of the main south wall of the fort, and a penetrating shot might have set off an explosion that would have destroyed much of the garrison. However, the Mexicans showed little interest in the south wall. Travis gave orders that the last man alive or the last to evacuate the fort was to fire the magazine if possible.

■ There was no shortage of firearms during the Alamo siege. Every man on the parapets had several loaded rifles, muskets, or pistols at his side. Many of the volunteers had brought more than one with them. According to *Three Roads to the Alamo*, there were 816 rifles, shotguns, pistols, and English Brown Bess muskets, almost four apiece for the garrison. There were also more than 15,000 prepared cartridges of powder and ball, most of them for the muskets, enough for 60 rounds or more per man.

■ What they didn't lack in firearms, the Alamo garrison lacked in proper artillery ammunition. They did not have enough to keep the enemy from reaching the walls. The gunners had enough powder to fire more than 1,200 rounds, but the 686 solid shot were all but useless against attacking infantry. Travis had less than 500 grape and canister loads to beat back the enemy assault.

■ Travis fired the 18-pounder three times a day beginning on March 3. The discharge was a signal. Any Texian hearing that gun would know that the men in the Alamo still held out.

■ The Alamo fell on the morning of March 6, 1836. In the words of General Filisola, ". . .by grapeshot, musketshot and the bayonet, they were all killed at last."

Other Fields of Battle

■ The legendary Gonzales cannon was a small six-pounder, shorter than a man's arm and weighed less than 70 pounds. In September 1835, Colonel Ugartecha attempted to reclaim the cannon which had been given to the people of Gonzales four years earlier. The colonists decided to fight rather than surrender the gun. They mounted it on a pair of cart wheels made from two slices of tree trunks, while townspeople gathered metal scraps to substitute for canister. Texians raised a white banner in defiance, a white cloth with an image of the disputed cannon barrel in black paint. Underneath appeared the challenge: COME AND TAKE IT." The small cannon fired the first shot of the Texas Revolution and was instrumental in winning the battle. The Gonzales cannon met its end on the march to San Antonio. The cannon was mounted on a cart drawn by four oxen. The axles and hubs began to smoke and they were forced to abandon the little piece of artillery at Sandy Creek. It had served the Texians well.

■ On April 11, two cannons arrived from Texas sympathizers in Cincinnati, Ohio. The pieces, later dubbed the "Twin Sisters," saw action at the Battle of San Jacinto. When the Texas army was within two hundred yards of the Mexican camp, Sam Houston ordered the Twin Sisters turned around. The two cannons were loaded with chopped horseshoes and discharged. The scrap-iron rain wreaked havoc on the sleeping Mexicans.

The Army of Operations

■ Most of the Mexican infantrymen were armed with British Brown Bess muskets. Although heavy, they were generally reliable and not significantly inferior to the muskets shouldered by most of the Texians.

■ Elite companies of the Mexican army were issued the British Baker Rifle. This was the first practical military rifle, since it could be fitted with a bayonet and had a rate of fire twice that of other rifles in use.

■ Marksmanship, per se, did not exist in Santa Anna's Mexican army since the soldiers were not trained to aim their muskets. Their Brown Bess weapons were heavy and produced quite a kick. In order to compensate, the Mexicans undercharged (used less powder) their shots, which reduced the musket's range. They further spared their shoulders by firing from the hip. Santa Anna's men were notorious for shooting five or even ten feet above their targets.

■ The only tactic that most of the Mexican soldiers knew was the frontal attack. Men fired from their weapons from their hips as they advanced and then closed with the bayonet. This was not an effective tactic against the more experienced Texians.

■   Santa Anna's expedition during the Texas campaign did not lack firepower. His army transported 21 pieces of heavy artillery, including two 12-caliber cannons and four eight-caliber cannons, and every soldier carried a firearm. The 12-pounders, however, straggled weeks behind the vanguard and played no role in the siege of the Alamo. Santa Anna relied on his nine-pounders as his workhorse artillery. Each weighed two tons and could fire two aimed rounds of solid shot per minute to a distance of 1,400 yards.

■   According to General Filisola, Mexican bullets caused the majority of Mexican casualties at the Alamo. Less than one quarter of them, he claimed, were caused by enemy fire.

Stephen F. Austin, The Father of Texas. Why did the reluctant revolutionary become a hardened advocate of war? *Texas State Library & Archives Commission.*

Chapter Eight

Officers and Gentlemen

Although the war's battles were fought by soldiers, events were shaped by men who never shouldered a musket. Texians and Mexicans, officers and gentlemen, soldiers and civilians, these men played a significant role in determining the outcome of the Texas Revolution.

■ Stephen F. Austin (1793-1836)

Stephen Austin set aside family and personal gain "to redeem Texas from its wilderness state by means of the plow alone. . ." Austin devoted his life to the colonists and to Texas. After his father, Moses Austin, died, Stephen carried on his father's work as Texas' first and most successful *empresario* (land agent) and eventually settled over 1,000 families.

Austin's first colony, "The Old Three Hundred," was being settled as early as November 1821, near Washington-on-the-Brazos and Columbus. Austin worked to integrate the American settlers into Mexican society. He served for a time in the Coahuila-Texas legislature, and as a member of various commissions and delegations. He sincerely believed that Texas ought to remain a part of Mexico, and worked hard toward establishing a separate state of Texas within Mexico.

In 1833, Austin traveled to Mexico City at the insistence of the colonists. He carried a petition to be delivered to the new president, Antonio López de Santa Anna, requesting that Texas and Coahuila be recognized as separate states. Austin was arrested on suspicion of inciting rebellion in Texas. He was imprisoned in Mexico City for eighteen months, and spent part of this time in solitary confinement. Austin became convinced there could not be a peaceful resolution. Upon his release, he sent a circular letter on September 19, 1835, throughout the colonies: "War is our only resource—there is no other remedy but to defend our rights, our country, and ourselves by force of arms."

Austin was elected Provisional President of Texas and named commander of the Texian forces. General Austin was appointed a commissioner in December 1835 and was sent to seek aid from the United States. Austin died December 27, 1836, in his two-room clapboard shack at Columbia while serving as Secretary of State under the new republic. "Texas" was among his last words.

After Austin's death, the President of the Texas Republic, Sam Houston, issued a proclamation which read in part: "The Father of Texas is no more! The first pioneer of the wilderness has departed!"

■ James Butler Bonham (1807-1836)

Responding to a call for volunteers to aid the Texas Revolution, James Butler Bonham, a South Carolina aristocrat and lawyer, held a rally in Mobile, Alabama on October 17, 1835. He organized the Mobile Grey Volunteers and struck out for Texas, and the column arrived in San Antonio on December 12.

Travis twice sent Bonham out of the Alamo with dispatches through enemy lines. The South Carolinian returned both times at great personal risk. Bonham was the last courier to return and tradition has it that he brought news to Travis that no aid was coming. In fact, evidence indicates that Bonham brought a letter from Willie Williamson which promised help from the colonies and claimed that Colonel Fannin was on the way with a relief force. Furthermore, Travis' letter of March 3, 1836, written after Bonham returned the second time, states, "Colonel Fannin is said to be on the march to this place with reinforcements; but I fear it is not true, as I have repeatedly sent to him for aid without receiving any. . . .I look to the colonies alone for aid."

Bonham reportedly met his death on the east wall of the Alamo church.

"I will report the result of my mission to Travis or die in the attempt." *James B. Bonham to Benjamin Highsmith, March 1, 1836.*

■ James Bowie (1795-1836)

A legend in his own time, James Bowie was born in Kentucky and moved to Missouri at the age of four, and again to Louisiana three years later. Often working with his brothers, he farmed, logged, roped and rode alligators, and made a fortune smuggling slaves with Jean Laffite and engaging in fraudulent land deals. Opportunities in land and tales of silver brought Bowie to Texas. Though he found no silver mincs, he did find his destiny.

By 1830 Bowie had settled in San Antonio, where he cultivated friendships with the elite of Tejano society. That same year he married Ursula Veramendi, daughter of the vice-governor of Coahuila and Texas. Bowie became a Mexican citizen and gained control of some 750,000 acres through land grants and purchases. Tragedy struck when Ursula and her parents died in 1833 during a cholera epidemic while Bowie was in Mississippi on business.

Although Bowie never enlisted and held no formal commission, he joined the Texas volunteers in 1835. He fought in the Battle at Concepción on October 28, in the Grass Fight on November 26, and in the Battle of Béxar on December 5-9, 1835.

Colonel Bowie arrived at the Alamo on January 19, 1836. He was convinced that the mud fort should be defended, as it was the only outpost between the colonists and the Mexicans. He immediately set about fortifying the Alamo with Green B. Jameson, the Alamo's chief engineer, at his side. Bowie wrote to Governor Henry Smith on February 2, ". . .we will rather die in these ditches than give it up to the enemy."

The Alamo's commander, Colonel James C. Neill, was called home and command was turned over to Lieutenant Colonel William Barret Travis as senior officer of the regular army. The volunteers, however, preferred the leadership of the Bowie—the "best known fighter in Texas"—and the problem was eventually resolved with Travis and Bowie sharing joint command of the mission.

Bowie had been sick for weeks and collapsed on or about February 24. Bowie wisely and publicly turned over his responsibilities to Colonel Travis. Bowie asked to be carried to a small room on the south side of the Alamo, where he remained throughout the siege. During the battle, Mexican soldiers found him in his bed and shot him.

Receiving the news of her son's death, Mrs. Rezin Bowie, Sr. supposedly stated, "So Jim is dead?. . .I'll wager they found no wounds in his back."

■ David Crockett (1786-1836)

The great frontiersman David Crockett was born in rural Tennessee, the son of a Revolutionary War veteran. Crockett married, had three children and took up farming. He volunteered for the Creek War of 1813-1814, serving under Andrew Jackson. His wife died in 1815, but he married a young widow with two children of her own.

Crockett was not a much of a success as a farmer or businessman, but he managed to make a name for himself in local politics. He was elected to a magistracy and served in the state legislature (1821-1825). He also served three terms in Congress, but left Tennessee in October 1835 after being defeated for a fourth term. The Honorable David Crockett reportedly told his constituents, "You may all go to hell and I will go to Texas."

In spite of his active involvement in politics, Crockett found time to disappear into the woods for extended periods of time and wrote tales about his adventures. He claimed to have killed 108 bears in one eight-month period.

Crockett arrived in Nacogdoches in January and helped organize the Tennessee Company of Mounted Volunteers. "I have come to your country, though not, I hope through any selfish motive whatever. I have come to aid you all that I can in your noble cause. I shall identify myself with your noble interests, and all the honor that I desire is that of defending as a high private, in common with my fellow citizens, the liberties of our common country."

Crockett and his company rode out for the Alamo and arrived on the 7th or 8th of February, 1836. Crockett's fame preceded him and his arrival was met with great excitement. He was immediately called on to speak. "I have come to your country, though not, I hope through any selfish motive whatever. I have come to aid you all that I can in your noble cause. I shall identify myself with your noble interests, and all the honor that I desire is that of defending as a high private, in common with my fellow citizens, the liberties of our common country."

At least one account records that Crockett reported to Colonel Travis and said, "Colonel, here am I. Assign us to some place, and I and my Tennessee boys will defend it." Crockett and his men were assigned to the weakest part of the wall—the palisade on the southwest side of the former church.

There is probably more controversy and speculation concerning Crockett's death than any other single event of the Texas Revolution. While some accounts claim that Crockett went down fighting, clubbing the Mexicans as he fell, other contemporary accounts claim he was one of a handful of prisoners saved by General Castrillión only to be executed at Santa Anna's orders. David Crockett died at the Alamo. That is all we know for certain.

■ Gregorio Esparza (1802-1836)

Gregorio Esparza joined Capt. Juan Seguin's company in October 1835. He fought with fellow Texians in the Battle of Béxar while his brother, Francisco, served in the Mexican army under General Cós.

Gregorio, a native of San Antonio, brought his wife Ana and their four children into the Alamo on the evening of February 23, climbing up through a small window in the church. Gregorio manned a cannon at the south window of the chapel, where he fell mortally wounded on March 6.

After the battle, Francisco obtained General Santa Anna's permission to recover his brother's body, and it was buried in the Campo Santo cemetery—the only defender to receive a Christian burial.

Gregorio's son, Enrique, survived the battle and later gave one of the few eyewitness accounts of the fight.

■ James Walker Fannin (1804-1836)

James Walker Fannin attended West Point in 1819. He apparently did not find the military academy to his liking and ran away in 1821 at a time when he stood 60th in a class of 86. Fannin eventually settled in Georgia, where he married and had two children. In 1834, he took his wife and two infant children to Velasco, Texas, where he became a successful land speculator and slave trader.

Fannin became one of the leaders of the "War Party" and spent part of the winter of 1834-1835 in the United States seeking support for an independent Texas. Fannin took part in several of the early actions of the War for Independence, including the battles at Gonzales on October 2, 1835, Concepción on October 28, and the capture of San Antonio in December. Fannin was promoted to colonel and was placed in command of an army gathering at Goliad.

Colonel Travis repeatedly looked to Colonel Fannin and his 400-450 men for relief of the Alamo. Despite numerous pleas for help, Fannin was unable or unwilling to send support and believed he was justified in his decision.

Following the fall of the Alamo, Houston ordered Fannin to evacuate Goliad. Fannin delayed his retreat and mismanaged the withdrawal. He and his men finally moved out on March 19, 1836. Only a few miles from the fort, near Coleto Creek, Fannin was completely surrounded by General Jose Urrea's superior numbers. A brief battle ensued, but the Texians were trapped on an open prairie without food or water and they surrendered the next morning.

The prisoners were marched to Goliad. On March 27, some 342 prisoners were marched out of Goliad and shot and stabbed to death by their guards. Back at Goliad, Fannin was blindfolded and shot in the head.

"What must be the feelings of the volunteers now shut in Béxar. . .
will not curses be heaped on the heads of the sluggards who remained
at home?"   *Colonel James Fannin to Lieutenant Governor Robinson,
February 28, 1836*

■ Samuel P. Houston (1793-1863)

Sam Houston was born in Virginia but his mother moved the
family to Tennessee after the death of his father in 1807. Houston ran
off to join the Indians and lived for three years with the Cherokee,
who called him "The Raven." In 1813, Houston volunteered for service in the war with Britain. He enlisted in the 7th Infantry and was
eventually promoted to lieutenant. He was wounded several times
during his five years in the army, once so severely that it troubled him
for the rest of his life. Houston formed lifelong friendships with both
David Crockett and Andrew Jackson. He resigned his commission in
1818 rather than take part in the forced removal of Indians from the
territory. Houston later became an Indian agent among the Cherokee
while studying law. He was admitted to the Tennessee bar, became a
major general of militia, and was elected to Congress in 1823 and
again in 1825. In 1827, he was elected governor of Tennessee. Two
years later he married Eliza Allen, a young girl still in her teens. For
reasons never made public, his wife left him and returned to her father's home four months later. Soon afterwards, Houston resigned his
governorship and headed west.

Houston settled among the Cherokee in Arkansas, where they had
recently been removed. His heavy drinking earned him the name
"Big Drunk." Houston married Tiana Rogers, a Cherokee woman and
reportedly gave up drinking. By 1832, he was making his way to
Texas.

In 1835, Sam Houston was made a major general and commander of the revolutionary army. Texas declared its independence on
Houston's birthday, March 2, 1836. A short time later, Major General
Houston led the revolutionary army to victory at San Jacinto on April
21, 1836.

Three months later he was elected President of the Republic of Texas. He served two terms as President (1836-1838 and 1841-1844). When Texas was admitted to the Union, Houston was elected to the United States Senate, serving until 1859, when he was elected governor of Texas.

Houston openly opposed secession and believed it would be a disaster for the South. In the face of strong opposition, he remained staunchly Unionist in a state that was heavily secessionist. In March 1861, he refused to endorse the Ordinance of Secession and refused to take the oath of allegiance to the Confederacy. As a result, he was removed from office by an illegal proceeding. Houston died on July 26, 1863, survived by a wife and eight children.

"Texas has achieved her entire independence, and successfully asserted her right to a position amidst the nations of the earth. . . .How has this been accomplished? By the spirit and energy of her citizens—by the valor of her sons—by the inspired language patriotism breathed by her daughters."   *General Sam Houston, President-elect, Houston, November 25, 1841*

■ Samuel Augustus Maverick (1803-1870)

Thirty-two-year-old Sam Maverick reached San Antonio in the fall of 1835 only to be arrested shortly thereafter by Mexican officers on suspicion of communicating with the Texian forces. He escaped and joined the Texas volunteers and fought in the Battle of Béxar in December 1835. On February 5, 1836, Sam Maverick was elected as one of two delegates to the Convention at Washington-on-the Brazos, where he signed the Declaration of Independence.

Maverick served as mayor of San Antonio from 1839 to 1840, and was captured along with fifty-two other prominent citizens by an invading Mexican force in September 1842. Maverick was imprisoned in the castle of Perote and released in March 1843. He returned to San Antonio and built his own home on Alamo property in 1849. In 1861, Maverick was one of the Texas commissioners for the

Confederate cause who demanded the surrender of the U.S. munitions of war–including the quartermaster's stores in the Alamo.

Sam Maverick served the Republic and the state many years in the legislature and yet another term as mayor of San Antonio. He was a successful speculator in land, and he generously gave large chunks of it for parks and churches in San Antonio.

"To the inheritors of his name," said his friend, Dr. George Cupples, "he has bequeathed a heritage richer than broad lands, more precious than fine gold—the name of a just, an upright and conscientious man."

■ Benjamin Rush Milam (1788-1835)

Ben Milam had lived a life of adventure. He left his home in Kentucky to fight in the War of 1812. Six years later he was on his way to Texas to trade goods with the Comanches. After stints as a sea captain, a Mexican soldier, a miner, and an empressario (land agent), he became a scout and volunteer in the Texian army.

Milam arrived in Goliad in October 1835 at the beginning of the Texas Revolution. He took part in the attack on the Mexican garrison at Goliad, where the Texians won a decisive victory by capturing the garrison and its valuable supplies. After the battle Milam took command of a company of scouts.

The Kentucky native returned from a scouting mission on December 4, 1835, and found the Texian army camped in the outskirts of San Antonio ready to withdraw. Milam's call to attack kept the army together and his death on the third day of battle helped rally the troops to victory at the Battle of Béxar. Colonel Ben Milam was the first hero of the Texas Revolution.

"As bright as thy example, so bright shall be thy fame.
And Generations yet unborn shall honor Milam's name."
From a poem by Erastus "Deaf" Smith, Columbia, Texas 1836

■ José Antonio Navarro (1795-1871)

Texas patriot José Antonio Navarro was one of four delegates from San Antonio to the Convention of 1836. He and his uncle, Francisco Ruiz, were the only native-born Texans to sign the Declaration of Independence. A prominent citizen of San Antonio, Navarro practiced law and managed both a general store and his family's ranch. He had served as a representative from San Antonio to the Mexican congress of Coahuila and Texas.

Navarro was imprisoned in 1841 for his participation in the Santa Fe Expedition of 1841. He spent three and one-half years in a Mexican dungeon, where he was under constant pressure to foreswear his allegiance to Texas. This he refused to do.

Navarro escaped from prison and helped write the Constitution of the State of Texas, which was accepted by the United States on December 29, 1845. José Antonio Navarro was elected to serve in the first Texas senate. He died in 1871.

■ Juan Nepomuceno Seguín (1806-1890)

Juan Nepomucena Seguín came from a wealthy and influential family. His father had been the alcalde (mayor) of San Antonio several times and had helped draft the liberal Constitution of 1824. Like his father, Juan also served as alcalde a number of times, the first when he was only 18 years old. He also served in the Coahuila-Texas state legislature and the Mexican Congress. A friend of American settlers in Texas, Seguín was active in the movement to make Texas a separate state and later joined the independence movement.

When the revolution broke out, Seguín organized Mexican ranchers along the lower San Antonio River into a cavalry unit. He served as a scout during the Battle of Concepción in October 1835, and again at the Battle of Béxar that December. His actions earned him a commission as a captain of cavalry in the Regular Texas Army. Seguín served as a messenger during the siege of the Alamo and was sent out on the night of February 25-26.

After the Alamo fell, Sequín commanded the rear guard when the Texian army under Houston began its retreat eastward. During the

Battle of San Jacinto, Seguín commanded the Ninth Company, Second Regiment of the Texas Volunteers, and was soon thereafter promoted to colonel. He was assigned command of the San Antonio area but had problems with the newly arrived settlers, who disputed his authority and generally abused Tejanos. While in San Antonio, Seguín paid final honors of war to the remains of the Alamo heroes.

Seguín was elected to the Texas senate in 1838 but resigned in 1840 when he was elected Mayor of San Antonio. His defense of Tejano rights led to charges that he was in treasonous correspondence with the Mexican army and collaborated in Mexican raids across the border. Seguín was forced from office in 1842. Fearing for his life, he took his family and fled to Mexico, where he was promptly arrested. He was impressed into the Mexican army and served as an officer against Texas during the continuing border troubles and later against the United States during the Mexican-American War. After the U.S.-Mexican peace settlement, Seguín received permission to return to the United States. He remained until 1867, and once again traveled south to Mexico.

Seguin, Texas, thirty-six miles east of San Antonio, was named for Juan Seguín in 1839. He died in 1890 and was buried in Nuevo Laredo, Mexico. His body was returned to Texas in 1974 and was reinterred in the town of Seguin two years later.

"Texas shall be free, and independent. Or. . .we will die gloriously in combat, toward that effort." *Juan Seguín, San Antonio, February 25, 1837*

■ Erastus "Deaf" Smith (1787-1837)

Hard of hearing since childhood, "Deaf" Smith was destined to become the greatest scout of the Texas Revolution. Smith came to Texas by way of Mississippi and arrived in San Antonio in 1821. He married a widow, Guadalupe Ruiz de Duran, and made many friends among the Mexicans. For that reason he was reluctant to get involved with the problems between the colonists and Mexico until General Martín de Perfecto Cós refused to let him enter San Antonio to see his wife and children. Thereafter Smith offered his services to Stephen

Austin and joined the Texian army. Deaf fought with James Fannin and James Bowie at the Battle of Concepción in October 1835, and led Colonel Frank Johnson's troops into San Antonio at the Battle of Béxar, December 1835.

Smith was returning from moving his family to safety when he stopped in Gonzales and learned of the fall of the Alamo. Houston sent him to San Antonio to gather information. En route he met Mrs. Susanna Dickenson and her baby and escorted them back to Houston's camp in Gonzales.

Houston made Deaf Smith commander of scouts and gave him the most dangerous reconnoitering and spying missions. On the morning of April 21, he destroyed the bridge over Vince's Bayou, a dangerous task which cut off the only route of retreat for the Mexican forces. After San Jacinto, Smith commanded an early unit of Texas Rangers, but his health was poor and he died in 1837. The Republic of Texas paid his wife a pension of $500 a year when they discovered Smith had died penniless.

"So valiantly and trustworthy was he, that all titles sink into insignificance before the simple name DEAF SMITH." *Taken from the Deaf Smith Monument, Richmond, Texas*

■ John William Smith (1792-1845)

John William Smith left Missouri in 1826 and headed for Texas with his brother Francis as part of Green DeWitt's Colony. In 1827, he moved to San Antonio and was appointed military storekeeper. He worked as a surveyor and civil engineer, and was the town's leading carpenter. Over six feet tall, with reddish-brown hair, Smith was soon known as "El Colorado" (The Redhead). In keeping with the Mexican colonization laws, he joined the Catholic faith in 1828 and married Maria de Jesús Curbelo in 1831.

Smith had not taken sides with Mexico or the colonists until he was arrested in the fall of 1835 on suspicion of communicating with the Texian army. Smith escaped and joined General Edward Burleson's army of volunteers. He drew a detailed map of San

Antonio and served as a guide in the Battle of Béxar in December 1835.

On February 23, 1836, Smith rode with Dr. John Sutherland to verify the sentry's sighting of Santa Anna's advance guard. That same afternoon Colonel Travis sent these men to Gonzales for reinforcements. At 3:00 p.m. on the morning of March 1, Smith guided the volunteers from Gonzales into the Alamo. On March 3, Travis again summoned Smith to carry a message, this time to the convention meeting at Washington-on-the-Brazos. Smith completed a daring ride through enemy lines, riding over 200 miles in less than fifty-seven hours, and thus escaped death in the Alamo.

In 1837, Smith was elected the first mayor of San Antonio. He served again from 1840 to 1844. In 1842, he gathered valuable information for the Republic during the Mexican invasion. Smith died of pneumonia in 1845 while serving as a senator from the Béxar (San Antonio) District in the Republic of Texas.

"A man of correct habits and principals and of a good moral character." *Citizens of Hannibal, Missouri, 1826*

■ William Barret Travis (1809-1836)

William Barret Travis was born in South Carolina but moved to Alabama as a child. Well educated for his day, he taught school for a time, read law and was admitted to the Alabama bar shortly before he turned 20. Travis married, practiced law and published a little newspaper, the *Claiborne Herald*, with the motto "Thou Shalt Not Muzzle the Ox That Treadeth out the Corn." He joined the militia and became a Mason.

Travis left his wife (who was pregnant with their second child) in 1831 and headed for Texas. Much speculation surrounds his reasons for leaving. One story claims that he killed a man who had made advances to his wife, while another claims he ran away from debt.

Travis settled first in Anahuac, then in San Felipe, where he acquired a reputation as a lawyer, gentleman, gambler, and womanizer. The dashing Travis wore a white hat and rode a black Spanish mare.

Although there were ten men for every woman in Texas, Travis found no shortage of women. He kept a meticulous diary with detailed records of his romantic conquests.

A member of the War Party, Travis became involved in the trouble between the colonists and Mexico, and led a march in June 1835 on the Mexican garrison at Anahuac, demanding its surrender and angering Santa Anna. Many view this event as the opening salvo of the Texas Revolution.

Commissioned a lieutenant colonel in the "Cavalry Corps" at the outbreak of the Texas Revolution, Travis was sent to San Antonio to reinforce the Alamo. Travis arrived on February 3, 1836, with thirty volunteers. He become convinced of the importance of defending the Alamo and wrote the governor, "It is more important to occupy this Post than I imagined when I last saw you—It is the key to Texas. "

When he left the garrison on February 13, the commander of the Alamo, Colonel James C. Neill, turned command over to Lieutenant Colonel Travis as senior officer of the Regular Army. The volunteers preferred Jim Bowie as their leader, and the problem was resolved when Travis and Bowie agreed to share joint command. Travis assumed full command of the Alamo when Bowie became ill later that month.

The Texians occupied and defended the fort during the twelve-day siege by an overwhelming Mexican force. Though Travis sent repeated appeals for help—to Fannin, to Houston, to the President of the Convention, and to "The People of Texas and All Americans in the world"—only thirty-two men from Gonzales are known to have responded. His letter to "The People of Texas and All Americans in the world" is considered one of the masterpieces of American patriotism. Much of what we know about the Texas side of the Alamo story is taken from the letters Travis wrote during the siege.

Ironically, Travis was one of the first to fall. He was defending the Alamo's north wall early on March 6 when he was struck in the forehead by a bullet. He fell back against one of the cannon and died, still clutching his gun.

■ **Lorenzo de Zavala (1788-1836)**

Originally educated for the priesthood, Zavala left the seminary and became a physician instead. He was an ardent liberal and became an important political figure while still in his mid-20s, serving in various municipal and regional posts.

Zavala was a member of the assembly of 1823-1824, which drew up the liberal Federal Constitution of 1824. He was elected to the first Senate in 1824 and governor of the State of Mexico in 1827, a post he resigned to become Minister of Finance.

Zavala received a grant to settle 500 families in the 1829. He did not act on this grant for some time as he went into exile after conservative Anastacio Bustamente took power later that same year. He spent the next three years in Europe and the United States. Returning to Mexico in 1832, he was elected to Congress and then as governor of Mexico once again. In 1833 President Santa Anna, allegedly federalist and liberal, made Zavala Minister to France. However, as Santa Anna moved to a centralist position, Zavala broke with him and resigned his post. He went to Texas in 1835 and soon became one of the most active revolutionary leaders. Zavala took part in the "Consultation" of October-November 1835 and was a signer of the Texas Declaration of Independence. He was elected vice-president in the provisional government of the Republic, but resigned due to ill health in October and died soon after.

Zavala's eldest son, also named Lorenzo, served in the Texas cavalry during the Revolution. Zavala's granddaughter, Adina, was a noted preservationist and historian.

SANTA ANNA AND HIS MEN

■ **Antonio López de Santa Anna Perez de Lebron (1794-1876)**

In 1810, shortly after the beginning of the War for Mexican Independence, 14-year-old Santa Anna enlisted as a cadet in the Regiment of Vera Cruz. He served with some distinction, rising to lieutenant of Grenadiers by 1815. Six years later he had risen to lieutenant colonel and was attached to the staff of General Agustín Iturbide. In 1821, Santa Anna was among those who urged Iturbide to proclaim the independence of Mexico. As a reward he was made a brigadier general at the age of 27.

Santa Anna helped write the widely admired Federal Constitution of 1824 and immediately went into retirement. He dominated Mexican politics for the next 30 years, sometimes as President and sometimes as rebel.

From the time Mexico declared its independence from Spain in 1821 until 1836, Mexico had one emperor and 11 presidents—one of which was a self-proclaimed dictator. General Santa Anna promised democracy but once he gained power in 1835, he named himself dictator. He abolished the Constitution of 1824 and imposed in its place a centralist document. This was one of the primary causes of the Texas Revolution. He shortly thereafter resigned the presidency in order to prosecute the Texas war more effectively.

As President of Mexico and general-in-chief of the Army of Operations, Santa Anna personally directed the siege of the Alamo. The victorious Santa Anna went on to preside over a stunning defeat at San Jacinto. He nearly escaped capture by running away and disguising himself in common soldier's clothes. However, he was apprehended and brought back to camp, where he was recognized by his own men. Houston spared Santa Anna's life in exchange for his promise to send his army home.

Santa Anna was in exile in 1846 when the Mexican War broke out. He returned to Mexico with American help and became President yet again. Taking up arms against the Americans, Santa Anna suffered disastrous defeats at the hands of Zachary Taylor and Winfield Scott, but these had little effect on his political career. He returned and regained the presidency one final time in 1853, only to be ousted two years later and sent into exile. Late in life he was permitted to return to Mexico, where he spent his last few years at his beloved hacienda above Vera Cruz.

The self-styled "Napoleon of the West," Santa Anna was fond of pretty women and had numerous affairs. He liked good living and wore three shirt studs worth over $5,000. He traveled with his own striped marquee, monogrammed china, crystal decanters, and silver

Antonio López de Santa Anna, The self-styled Napoleon of the West. Was Santa Anna caught unawares at San Jacinto because he was taking a siesta or was he engaged in a tryst with the Yellow Rose of Texas?
Texas State Library & Archives Commission.

chamber pot. He carried a $7,000 sword and rode a saddle decorated with gold-plated trim. Santa Anna indulged often in opium, wagered enormous sums at cockfighting, and wielded power with indifference to its consequences. He died in Mexico on June 22, 1876.

"If I were God, I would wish to be more."
Antonio López de Santa Anna

■ Juan Nepomuceno Almonte (1803-1869)

The illegitimate son of the Mexican revolutionary hero Father José Morelos, Juan Nepomuceno Almonte was no stranger to war. He was educated in a Catholic school in New Orleans, where he became fluent in English. With the establishment of an independent Mexico, he returned home and embarked upon a long and successful career as a soldier, diplomat, and politician.

During the Texas campaign, Almonte served as an aide to Santa Anna and was captured at San Jacinto. His memoirs of the campaign are among the most valuable sources of information on the operations of the Mexican army.

Almonte served as Mexican Minister in Washington in the mid-1840s until the U.S. annexed Texas in 1845. He did not hold any important command during the Mexican-American War, and thereafter returned to politics. Almonte was President of Mexico from April through September of 1862. He helped engineer the French intervention and subsequently served Emperor Maximilian faithfully, rising to Lieutenant General of the Realm. He died in exile in Paris in 1869.

■ Manuel Fernandez Castrillón (178?-1836)

Manuel Fernandez Castrillón entered the Spanish Colonial Army and was eventually sent to Mexico. There, he served with distinction in various assignments, first in Royal service, helping to crush the Mexican Revolution, then with Iturbide's Imperial government and finally with the Republic, in the process rising to a brigadier general. A well-trained professional officer, Castrillón became one of Santa Anna's closest advisors and confidants.

Castrillón repeatedly argued for fair and humane treatment of prisoners of war. According to Jeff Long in *Duel of Eagles*, Castrillón had once been a prisoner of war himself following one of Santa Anna's failed coup attempts in 1832. Castrillón refused to flee the field when the Mexican army broke at San Jacinto. He fell bravely trying to rally the troops.

■ Martin Perfecto de Cós (1802-1854)

Martin Perfecto de Cós ran away from home at an early age to join the revolutionary forces under José Morelos. After Mexico won her independence, he passed into the new Regular Army and rose to the rank of brigadier general. Cós was one of Santa Anna's closest advisors for two reasons: he had married the general's sister in the early 1820s and he had enormous political influence in his native Tehuantepec.

President Santa Anna sent his brother-in-law to Texas in September 1835 with orders to expel all Americans who had come to Texas since 1830, to disarm the Texians and to arrest all Texas patriots opposing Santa Anna's regime. General Cós arrived in San Antonio with 21 pieces of artillery and an army of 1,200 men, divided into two divisions: one to occupy the Alamo and one to defend the barricades in the center of town.

General Cós suffered a humiliating loss to 300 Texas volunteers at the Battle of Béxar. In the terms of surrender, General Cós pledged not to serve further against Texas. Within two months he was back to command a column in the attack on the Alamo.

■ Vicente Filisola (1789-1850)

Vicente Filisola enlisted in the Spanish army in 1804 at the age of fifteen. By the time he was twenty-one, he had fought in over twenty battles and held the rank of second lieutenant. In 1811, he was shipped to Mexico to help put down the revolution which had broken out the previous year. He was promoted first lieutenant of light infantry in January of 1812, captain of artillery in June of 1813, and captain of grenadiers in May of 1814. Attached to Agustín Iturbide's command from early 1814, by 1821 Filisola was a lieutenant colonel commanding 4,000 men, the largest contingent of Royalist forces in Mexico.

When Iturbide made himself Emperor in late 1821, he made Filisola brigadier general and sent him to "liberate" Central America. Filisola returned to Mexico after the fall of Itrubide and was given various important assignments. He was promoted to major general in 1829 and was made President of the Supreme War Council in 1830 and a justice of the military appeals branch of the Supreme Court, which posts he held until January of 1833, when he was made commanding general of the eastern regions of Mexico. He became ill a short time later and retired from active service.

Santa Anna recalled Filisola to duty in November 1835. General Filisola was Santa Anna's most trusted general and served as his second-in-command during the Texas campaign. Filisola assumed command of the army after San Jacinto and obeyed Santa Anna's orders to withdraw from Texas, which brought him under severe censure from Santa Anna and other officers. The principal charge was that he should have disobeyed Santa Anna's orders since they were illegal, issued by an officer who was a prisoner-of-war. In *Texian Iliad*, Stephen Hardin points out that Filisola had compelling reasons for making the withdrawal. The foul weather made travel of any kind almost impossible, his supply lines were stretched to the breaking point, and his soldiers were on the verge of starvation and many were ill. They could expect no reinforcements, no ammunition, and no food. He cut his losses, preserved his force and took his men home.

Filisola was named commanding general of Tampico and Nueva Leon in 1837 and promoted to Commanding General of the Mexican army early in 1839. He was forced to leave this post in mid-1840 when he was imprisoned and subjected to a court martial concerning his activities after San Jacinto. He finally secured an acquittal in 1841, whereupon he retired. He was recalled to duty during the Mexican-American War and served with distinction in Chihuahua in late 1847. The following year he was once again named to the Supreme War Council, and served in this post until his death from cholera in July 1853.

■ José Vicente Miñon

General Miñon demonstrated courage on many fields. In 1822 he and thirty men withstood the onslaught of an enemy column in Jalapa. A decade later he led sixty men in a charge against 400 enemy cavalry troops. Soon thereafter, he and 120 men captured an enemy battalion of 350. Miñon and his soldiers were the first to enter San Antonio during the Texas campaign, and the first to gain the interior of the Alamo during the battle of March 6, 1836.

■ José Enrique de la Peña (1807-1841)

According to Jeff Long in *Duel of Eagles*, de la Peña was one of Santa Anna's best officers. He had been trained as a mining engineer but chose to make a career of the military. De la Peña fought Spanish invaders at Tampico in 1829. He was later assigned as a military attaché to a European legation, but managed to secure permission in the fall of 1835 to head north for Texas.

After his return from Texas, de la Peña supported General José Urrea's armed opposition to the Mexican central government. De la Peña hated Santa Anna and his famous "diary" was full of criticism. He accused Santa Anna of wasting the lives of his men in a needless attack on the Alamo. He also claimed that Santa Anna ordered the execution of David Crockett, whom de la Peña presents as an innocent bystander, along with six other survivors. His support of Urrea and his outspoken criticism of Santa Anna brought him prosecution and incarceration in a series of prisons. As a consequence his name was erased from every record of the campaign.

De la Peña's account of the Texas Campaign has been described as the best single source we have on the Alamo; others label it a complete fraud. Many of the events are very convincing in their detail, and some historians believe it is an authentic, if not completely accurate, history.

■ José Nicolas de la Portilla (1808-1873)

José Nicolas de la Portilla was imprisoned in the same cell as General Castrillión in 1832 when he was only a 24-year-old lieutenant. However, Portilla did not share General Castrillión's compassion. In fact he came to be known as a butcher. It was Portilla who personally oversaw the mass execution of 342 Texas prisoners of war at Goliad.

Portilla was promoted to colonel by the time he entered Texas and was under the command of General Jose Urrea. Portilla later served as the Mexican Minister of War and died in 1873.

■ **Juan José Urrea (1795-1849)**

Juan José Urrea was born in Tucson (in what is now Arizona), although his family had roots in Durango. He entered the Royal Army as a cadet at the age of twelve. His early military career was spent suppressing revolutionary outbreaks. Urrea was a captain by the time Mexico attained its independence. He left the army after the Spanish departed but returned to duty as a major in 1829, after the Spanish seized Tampico. He was promoted to lieutenant colonel in 1832 and to colonel upon Santa Anna's assuming the presidency. He was promoted to brigadier general in 1835 and sent to Durango to fight Apaches until Santa Anna called Urrea to duty in Texas.

Urrea commanded with considerable skill the independent division, which operated along the Texas coast. He was responsible for the series of defeats sustained by the Texas forces at San Patricio, Refugio, Goliad, and Coleto Creek, the latter of which resulted in the surrender of Fannin and his men. Urrea objected to Santa Anna's orders to execute all prisoners and managed to save many of them. He was one of the officers who urged Filisola to disobey Santa Anna's orders to evacuate Texas after San Jacinto.

After the Texas campaign, Urrea served as commanding general in Sonora and Sinaloa. He fell out completely with Santa Anna and raised his own command in 1837 in the name of a Federal Constitution, but was defeated at Mazatlan early the next year. He escaped and attempted a coup at Tampico, which also failed. Imprisoned, he escaped and was recaptured several times. Urrea was expelled from the army but returned during the "Pastry War." In 1840, he led an uprising against the Bustamente government but was defeated and fled to Durango. He rallied that region to the Federalist cause in 1841, helping to put the "born-again" Federalist Santa Anna into the presidency once more. Santa Anna named Urrea governor of Sonora, and he held various other civil and military posts thereafter. He successfully commanded a cavalry division in northern Mexico during the Mexican-American War, but also took part in the Mexican defeat at Buena Vista. General Urrea died of cholera shortly after the war ended.

Chapter Nine

Alamo Defenders

At least 183 men died defending the Alamo, although evidence suggests that as many as 250 to 260 lost their lives in the tragedy.

The defenders of the Alamo came from eighteen states and five European countries. Most were recent arrivals in Texas from the United States. At least twenty were born in Europe, with two from Germany and four from England. Only two or three had been in Texas as long as six years.

Remarkably, not one of the Alamo defenders was a professional soldier. Instead they were medical doctors, farmers, lawyers, clerks, and a Baptist preacher. And one, of course, was the greatest bear hunter in all the West.

Their average age was twenty-nine. The youngest was probably fifteen-year old William Philip King, one of the Gonzales Ranging Company. The oldest was fifty-five-year old Robert Moore, who came to Texas with the News Orleans Greys. Some had come to Texas to acquire land, some to escape family and financial problems, and some simply for the sake of adventure. But all shared a common bond: they were willing to fight and die for the cause of liberty.

"If we succeed, the country is ours, it is immense in extent and fertile in its soil and will amply reward all our toils. If we fail, death in the cause of liberty and humanity is not cause for shuddering. Our rifles are by our sides and choice guns they are; we know what awaits us and are prepared to meet it."

Daniel William Cloud to his brother,
San Antonio de Bexar, December 26, 1835

Much of the information on the defenders of the Texas mission was derived from Bill Groneman's Alamo Defenders. *The list has been changed and altered over the years. It is likely that ongoing research will uncover names of additional defenders not listed here.*

(Note: "From" denotes last known residence and not necessarily place of birth.)

■ **Juan Abamillo**, a resident and native of Texas, was a sergeant in Captain Juan N. Seguín's cavalry company. Sergeant Abamillo was killed at the Alamo.

■ **James L. Allen**, a twenty-one-year-old college student from Kentucky, served as a rifleman and courier. Private Allen carried a message out of the mission on March 5, 1836. He was the last courier to leave the Alamo.

■ **Robert Allen**, a native of Virginia, served as a rifleman in Captain Forsyth's cavalry company. Private Allen was killed at the Alamo.

■ **Miles DeForest Andross**, a twenty-seven-year-old resident of San Patricio, Texas, served as a rifleman with Captain Blazeby's infantry company. Private Andross was killed at the Alamo.

■ **Micajah Autry**, a forty-two-year-old farmer, teacher, lawyer, and shopkeeper from Tennessee, served as a rifleman with Captain William B. Harrison's company. Private Autry was killed at the Alamo.

■ **Juan Antonio Badillo**, a resident and native of Texas, served as a sergeant with Captain Seguín's cavalry company. Sergeant Badillo was killed at the Alamo.

■ **Peter James Bailey III,** a twenty-four-year-old lawyer from Kentucky, served as a rifleman with Captain Harrison's company. Private Bailey was killed at the Alamo.

■ **Isaac G. Baker**, a twenty-one-year-old volunteer from Gonzales, Texas, arrived with the Gonzales Ranging Company and served as a rifleman. Private Baker was killed at the Alamo.

■ **William Charles M. Baker**, a volunteer from Mississippi, held the rank of captain. It is believed he was the commanding officer of the volunteers who accompanied James Bowie back to the Alamo. Captain Baker was killed at the Alamo.

■ **John J. Ballentine**, a volunteer from Bastrop, Texas, served as an artilleryman with Captain Carey's artillery company. Private Ballentine was killed at the Alamo.

■ **Richard W. Ballentine**, a twenty-two-year-old volunteer from Alabama, served as a rifleman. Private Ballentine was killed at the Alamo.

■ **John J. Baugh**, a thirty-three-year-old volunteer from Virginia, held the rank of captain. As Travis' executive officer, Baugh assumed command of the Alamo after the death of Travis. Captain Baugh was killed at the Alamo.

■ **Joseph Bayliss**, a twenty-eight-year-old volunteer from Tennessee, served as a rifleman with Captain Harrison's company. Private Bayliss was killed at the Alamo.

■ **John Walker Baylor, Jr.,** a twenty-two-year-old doctor from Fort Gibson, Arkansas, served as a rifleman with Captain Dimmit's company. It is believed Private Baylor left the Alamo as a courier on February 25, 1836.

■ **John Blair**, a thirty-three-year-old volunteer from Zavala's Colony, Texas, served as a rifleman. Private Blair was killed at the Alamo.

■ **Samuel Blair**, a twenty-nine-year-old volunteer from McGloin's Colony, Texas. He held the rank of captain and was the assistant to the ordnance chief. Captain Blair was killed at the Alamo.

■ **William Blazeby**, a forty-one-year-old volunteer from New York, arrived in Texas with the New Orleans Greys. Captain Blazeby commanded an infantry company. He was killed at the Alamo.

■ **James Butler Bonham**, a twenty-nine-year-old lawyer from Montgomery, Alabama, held the rank of Second Lieutenant and served as a courier and rifleman. He left the Alamo twice to deliver messages and returned twice at great risk to himself. Lieutenant Bonham was killed at the Alamo.

■ **Daniel Bourne**, a twenty-six-year-old volunteer from Gonzales, Texas, served as an artilleryman with Captain Carey's artillery company. Private Bourne was killed at the Alamo.

■ **James Bowie**, a forty-year-old sugar planter, slave trader, and land speculator, was a resident of San Antonio. He held the rank of colonel and was the commander of the volunteer troops among the Alamo garrison and co-commander of the garrison from February 14–24, 1836. Bowie became incapacitated by an ongoing illness on February 24, and turned over full command to Travis. Colonel Bowie was killed at the Alamo.

■ **Jesse B. Bowman,** a fifty-one-year-old hunter and trapper from Red River County, Texas, served as a rifleman. Private Bowman was killed at the Alamo.

■ **George Brown**, a thirty-five-year-old volunteer from Gonzales, Texas, served as a rifleman. Private Brown was killed at the Alamo.

■ **James Brown**, a thirty-six-year-old volunteer from De Leon's Colony, Texas, served as a rifleman. Private Brown was killed at the Alamo.

■ **Robert Brown**, an eighteen-year-old volunteer from Texas, served as a rifleman, a raider and a courier. It is believed that Private Brown left the Alamo as a courier sometime after February 25, 1836.

■ **James Buchanan**, a twenty-three-year-old volunteer from Austin's Colony, Texas, served as a rifleman. Private Buchanan was killed at the Alamo.

■ **Samuel E. Burns**, a twenty-six-year-old volunteer from Louisiana, served as an artilleryman in Captain Carey's artillery company. Private Burns was killed at the Alamo.

■ **George D. Butler**, a twenty-three-year-old volunteer, came to Texas by way of New Orleans. Private Butler served as a rifleman and was killed at the Alamo.

■ **John Cain,** a thirty-four-year-old volunteer from Gonzales, Texas, arrived with the Gonzales Ranging Company and served as an artilleryman in Captain Carey's artillery company. Private Cain was killed at the Alamo.

■ **Robert Campbell**, a twenty-six-year-old volunteer from Tennessee, held the rank of Lieutenant in Captain Harrison's Company. Lieutenant Campbell was killed at the Alamo.

■ **William R. Carey**, a thirty-year-old volunteer from Washington-on-the-Brazos, Texas, held the rank of captain and commanded an artillery company. Captain Carey was killed at the Alamo.

■ **Charles Henry Clark**, a volunteer from Missouri, served as a rifleman. Private Clark was killed at the Alamo.

■ **M. B. Clark**, a volunteer and native of Mississippi, served as a rifleman. Private Clark was killed at the Alamo.

■ **Daniel W. Cloud**, a twenty-four-year-old lawyer from Kentucky, served as a rifleman with Captain Harrison's company. Private Cloud was killed at the Alamo.

■ **Robert E. Cochran**, a volunteer from Brazoria, Texas, served as an artilleryman with Captain Carey's artillery company. Private Cochran was killed at the Alamo.

■ **George Washington Cottle**, a twenty-five-year-old volunteer from DeWitt's Colony, Texas, arrived with the Gonzales Ranging Company. George Cottle was killed at the Alamo.

■ **Henry Courtman**, a twenty-eight-year-old volunteer from Germany, served as a rifleman. He came to Texas by way of New Orleans with the New Orleans Greys. Private Courtman was killed at the Alamo.

■ **Lemuel Crawford**, a twenty-two-year-old volunteer from South Carolina, served as an artilleryman in Captain Carey's artillery company. Private Crawford was killed at the Alamo.

■ **David Crockett**, a forty-nine-year-old former United States Congressman from Tennessee, served as a rifleman in Captain Harrison's company. Private Crockett was killed at the Alamo.

■ **Robert Crossman**, a twenty-six-year-old volunteer from Pennsylvania, served as a rifleman with Captain Blazeby's infantry company. Private Crossman was killed at the Alamo.

■ **Antonio Cruz y Arocha**, a resident of Mexico, served as an orderly and courier for Captain Seguín's cavalry company. Private Cruz y Arocha left the Alamo as a courier on February 25, 1836.

■ **David P. Cummings**, a twenty-seven-year-old surveyor from Pennsylvania, arrived with the Gonzales Ranging Company and served as a rifleman. Private Cummings was killed at the Alamo.

■ **Robert Cunningham**, a thirty-one-year-old flatboatman from Austin's Colony, Texas, served as an artilleryman in Captain Carey's artillery company. Private Cunningham was killed at the Alamo.

■ **Jacob C. Darst**, a forty-two-year-old farmer from Gonzales, Texas, arrived with the Gonzales Ranging Company and served as a rifleman. Private Darst was killed at the Alamo.

■ **John Davis**, a twenty-five-year-old volunteer from Gonzales, Texas, arrived with the Gonzales Ranging Company and served as a rifleman. Private Davis was killed at the Alamo.

■ **Freeman H. K. Day**, a thirty-year-old volunteer, served as a rifleman with Captain White's infantry company. Private Day was killed at the Alamo.

■ **Jerry C. Day**, a twenty-year-old volunteer from Gonzales, Texas, served as a rifleman. Private Day was killed at the Alamo.

■ **Squire Daymon**, a twenty-eight-year-old volunteer from Gonzales, Texas, arrived with the Gonzales Ranging Company. He served as an artilleryman in Captain Carey's artillery company. Private Daymon was killed at the Alamo.

■ **William Dearduff**, a volunteer from Gonzales, Texas, arrived with the Gonzales Ranging Company and served as a rifleman. Private Dearduff was killed at the Alamo.

■ **Alexandro de la Garza**, a resident of Texas, served as a rifleman and courier for Captain Seguín's cavalry company. Private de la Garza left the Alamo as a courier.

■ **Stephen Dennison**, a twenty-four-year-old glazer and painter from Kentucky, served as a rifleman with Captain Blazeby's infantry company. Private Dennison was killed at the Alamo.

■ **Francis L. DeSauque**, a merchant and storeowner from Matagorda, Texas, held the rank of Captain. Captain DeSauque left the Alamo on February 22 to obtain provisions.

■ **Charles Despallier**, a twenty-four-year-old volunteer from Louisiana, served as a rifleman, a raider, and a courier. He left the Alamo in the latter capacity after February 25, 1836, but returned with the Gonzales Ranging Company on March 1, 1836. Private Despallier was killed at the Alamo.

■ **Lewis Dewall**, a twenty-four-year-old plasterer, mason, boatman, and blacksmith from Vehlein's Colony, Texas, served as a rifleman with Captain White's infantry company. Private Dewall was killed at the Alamo.

■ **Almeron Dickenson**, a twenty-six-year-old blacksmith from Gonzales, Texas, served as an artillery officer and held the rank of captain. Almeron's wife, Susannah, was one of the Alamo survivors. Captain Dickenson was killed at the Alamo.

■ **John Henry Dillard**, a thirty-one-year-old volunteer from Nashville-on-the-Brazos, Texas, served as a rifleman. Private Dillard was killed at the Alamo.

■ **Philip Dimitt**, a thirty-five-year-old merchant from LaVaca Bay, Texas, held the rank of captain and served as a courier. Captain Dimitt left the Alamo as a courier on February 23, 1836.

■ **James R. Dimpkins**, a resident of England, came to Texas by way of New Orleans as a member of the New Orleans Greys. He held the rank of sergeant in Captain Blazeby's infantry company. Sergeant Dimpkins was killed at the Alamo.

■ **Andrew Duvalt**, a thirty-two-year-old plasterer from Gonzales, Texas, served as a rifleman with Captain White's infantry company. Private Duvalt was killed at the Alamo.

■ **Carlos Espalier**, a seventeen-year-old resident of San Antonio, Texas, served as a rifleman. Private Espalier was killed at the Alamo.

■ **José Gregorio Esparza**, a twenty-seven-year-old volunteer from San Antonio, Texas, served as an artilleryman with Captain Seguín's cavalry company. Private Esparza was killed at the Alamo.

■ **Robert Evans**, a thirty-six-year-old volunteer from New York, held the rank of major and served as the master of ordnance. Major Evans was killed at the Alamo.

■ **Samuel B. Evans**, a twenty-four-year-old volunteer from Kentucky, served as a rifleman. Private Evans was killed at the Alamo.

■ **James L. Ewing**, a twenty-four-year-old volunteer from Tennessee, served as an artilleryman and as secretary to the commanding officer in Captain Carey's artillery company. Private Ewing was killed at the Alamo.

■ **William Keener Fauntleroy**, a twenty-two-year-old volunteer from Kentucky, served as a rifleman with Captain Harrison's company. Private Fauntleroy was killed at the Alamo.

■ **William Fishbaugh**, a volunteer from Gonzales, Texas, arrived with the Gonzales Ranging Company and served as a rifleman. Private Fishbaugh was killed at the Alamo.

■ **John Flanders**, a thirty-six-year-old volunteer from Austin's Colony, Texas, arrived with the Gonzales Ranging Company and served as a rifleman. Private Flanders was killed at the Alamo.

■ **Dolphin Ward Floyd**, a thirty-two-year-old farmer from Gonzales, Texas, arrived with the Gonzales Ranging Company and served as a rifleman. Private Floyd was killed at the Alamo.

■ **John Hubbard Forsyth**, a thirty-eight-year-old farmer and former doctor from Kentucky, held the rank of captain and was the commanding officer of a cavalry company. Captain Forsyth was killed at the Alamo.

■ **Antonio Fuentes**, a twenty-three-year-old volunteer from San Antonio, Texas, served as a rifleman with Captain Seguín's cavalry company. Private Fuentes was killed at the Alamo.

■ **Galba Fuqua**, a sixteen-year-old volunteer from Gonzales, Texas, arrived with the Gonzales Ranging Company and served as a rifleman. Private Fuqua was killed at the Alamo.

■ **William Garnett**, a twenty-four-year-old Baptist preacher from Falls-on-the-Brazos, Texas, served as a rifleman. Private Garnett was killed at the Alamo.

■ **James W. Garrand**, a twenty-three-year-old volunteer from Louisiana, served as a rifleman with Captain Blazeby's infantry company. Private Garrand was killed at the Alamo.

■ **James Girard Garrett**, a thirty-year-old volunteer from Louisiana, served as a rifleman with Captain Blazeby's infantry company. Private Garrett was killed at the Alamo.

■ **John E. Garvin**, a twenty-seven-year-old volunteer from Gonzales, Texas, arrived with the Gonzales Ranging Company and served as an artilleryman with Captain Carey's artillery company. Private Garvin was killed at the Alamo.

■ **John E. Gaston**, a seventeen-year-old volunteer from Gonzales, Texas, arrived with the Gonzales Ranging Company and served as a rifleman. Private Gaston was killed at the Alamo.

■ **James George**, a thirty-four-year-old volunteer from Gonzales, Texas, arrived with the Gonzales Ranging Company and served as a rifleman. Private George was killed at the Alamo.

■ **John C. Goodrich**, a twenty-seven-year-old volunteer from Grimes County, Texas, held the rank of cornett and served as a company officer and guidon bearer, possibly with Captain Forsyth's cavalry company. Cornett Goodrich was killed at the Alamo.

■ **Albert Calvin Grimes**, an eighteen-year-old volunteer from Texas, served as a rifleman. Private Grimes was killed at the Alamo.

■ **Brigido Guerrero**, a former Mexican soldier and resident of San Antonio, Texas, apparently deserted the Mexican army and joined the Texas revolutionaries. Guerrero was discovered hiding in the Alamo chapel by Mexican soldiers. He managed to convince them that he was a prisoner of the Texians and had been unable to escape. Private Guerrero survived the battle of the Alamo.

■ **James C. Gwynne**, a thirty-two-year-old volunteer from Mississippi, served as an artilleryman with Captain Carey's artillery company. Private Gwynne was killed at the Alamo.

■ **James Hannum**, a twenty-year-old volunteer, served as a rifleman. Private Hannum was killed at the Alamo.

■ **John Harris**, a twenty-three-year-old volunteer from Gonzales, Texas, served as a rifleman with the Gonzales Ranging Company. Private Harris was killed at the Alamo.

■ **Andrew Jackson Harrison**, a twenty-seven-year-old volunteer, served as a rifleman. Private Harrison was killed at the Alamo.

■ **William B. Harrison**, a twenty-five-year-old volunteer from Tennessee, held the rank of captain. He served as the commanding officer of the Tennessee Mounted Volunteers. Captain Harrison was killed at the Alamo.

■ **Joseph M. Hawkins**, a thirty-seven-year-old volunteer from Louisiana, served as a rifleman. Private Hawkins was killed at the Alamo.

■ **John M. Hays**, a twenty-two-year-old volunteer from Tennessee, served as a rifleman. Private Hays was killed at the Alamo.

■ **Charles M. Heiskell**, a twenty-three-year-old volunteer, served as a rifleman. Private Heiskell was killed at the Alamo.

■ **Patrick Henry Herndon**, a thirty-four-year-old volunteer from Navidad, Texas, served as a rifleman. Private Herndon was killed at the Alamo.

■ **William Daniel Hersee,** a thirty-one-year-old volunteer from New York, held the rank of sergeant in Captain Carey's artillery company. Sergeant Hersee was killed at the Alamo.

■ **Benjamin Franklin Highsmith**, an eighteen-year-old volunteer from Bastrop, Texas, served as courier and left the Alamo just before the siege.

■ **Tapley Holland**, a twenty-six-year-old volunteer from Grimes County Texas, served as an artilleryman with Captain Carey's artillery company. Private Holland was killed at the Alamo.

■ **Samuel Holloway**, a twenty-eight-year-old volunteer, came to Texas by way of Louisiana with the New Orleans Greys. He served as a rifleman with Captain Blazeby's infantry. Private Holloway was killed at the Alamo.

■ **William D. Howell**, a forty-five-year-old doctor from New York, served as a rifleman with Captain Blazeby's infantry company. Private Howell was killed at the Alamo.

■ **Thomas Jackson,** a volunteer from Gonzales, Texas, arrived with the Gonzales Ranging Company and served as a rifleman. Private Jackson was killed at the Alamo.

■ **William Daniel Jackson**, a twenty-nine-year-old former sailor, served as an artilleryman with Captain Carey's artillery company. Private Jackson was killed at the Alamo.

■ **Green B. Jameson**, a twenty-nine-year-old lawyer from Brazoria, Texas, held the rank of major and served as a staff officer and chief engineer. Major Jameson was killed at the Alamo.

■ **Gordon C. Jennings**, a fifty-six-year-old farmer from Austin's Colony, Texas, held the rank of 1st corporal with Captain Carey's artillery company. Corporal Jennings was killed at the Alamo.

■ **Joe**, a twenty-one to twenty-three-year-old slave, accompanied Travis as his servant to the Alamo. Joe served as a rifleman but did not hold any rank. He survived the battle.

■ **John,** a store clerk and possibly a slave, served as a rifleman without rank. John was killed at the Alamo.

■ **Lewis Johnson**, a volunteer from Nacogdoches, Texas, may have served as an artilleryman with Captain Carey's artillery company. Private Johnson was killed at the Alamo.

■ **William Johnson**, a volunteer from Texas, may have served as an artilleryman in Captain Carey's artillery company. Private Johnson was killed at the Alamo.

■ **William P. Johnson** was a courier and possibly a sergeant. It is believed he left the Alamo as a courier on February 23, 1836.

■ **John Jones**, a twenty-six-year-old volunteer, came to Texas by way of New Orleans with the New Orleans Greys. He held the rank of 1st lieutenant and served as a company officer in Captain

Blazeby's infantry company. Lieutenant Jones was killed at the Alamo.

■ **John Benjamin Kellogg**, a nineteen-year-old volunteer from Gonzales, Texas, arrived with the Gonzales Ranging Company and served as a rifleman. Private Kellogg was killed at the Alamo.

■ **James Kenney**, a twenty-two-year-old volunteer from Washington-on-the-Brazos, Texas, served as a rifleman. Private Kenney was killed at the Alamo.

■ **Andrew Kent**, a thirty-four to thirty-eight-year-old farmer from Gonzales, Texas, arrived with the Gonzales Ranging Company and served as a rifleman. Private Kent was killed at the Alamo.

■ **Joseph Kerr**, a twenty-two-year-old volunteer from Louisiana, served as a rifleman. Private Kerr was killed at the Alamo.

■ **George C. Kimball**, a thirty-three-year-old volunteer from Gonzales, Texas, held the rank of lieutenant and served as the commanding officer of the Gonzales Ranging Company. Lieutenant Kimball was killed at the Alamo.

■ **William Philip King**, a fifteen-year-old volunteer from Gonzales, Texas, arrived with the Gonzales Ranging Company and served as a rifleman. Private King was killed at the Alamo.

■ **William Irvine Lewis**, a twenty-nine-year-old from Pennsylvania, served as a rifleman. Private Lewis was killed at the Alamo.

■ **William J. Lightfoot**, a twenty-five-year-old volunteer from Gonzales, Texas, held the rank of 3rd corporal in Captain

Carey's artillery company. Corporal Lightfoot was killed at the Alamo.

■ **Jonathan L. Lindley**, a twenty-two-year-old surveyor from Gonzales, Texas, arrived with the Gonzales Ranging Company and served as an artilleryman with Captain Carey's artillery company. Private Lindley was killed at the Alamo.

■ **William Linn**, a volunteer from Boston, Massachusetts, came to Texas with the New Orleans Greys. He served as a rifleman in Captain Blazeby's infantry company. Private Linn was killed at the Alamo.

■ **Byrd Lockhart**, a fifty-year-old surveyor from Gonzales, Texas, held the rank of Captain and served as a courier. Captain Lockhart left the Alamo shortly before the battle to obtain supplies for the garrison.

■ **Toribio Losoya**, a twenty-eight-year-old volunteer from San Antonio, Texas, served as a rifleman with Captain Seguín's cavalry company. Private Losoya was killed at the Alamo.

■ **George Washington Main**, a twenty-nine-year-old volunteer, held the rank of lieutenant in Captain White's infantry company. Lieutenant Main was killed at the Alamo.

■ **William T. Malone**, an eighteen-year-old from Alabama, served as an artilleryman with Captain Carey's artillery company. Private Malone was killed at the Alamo.

■ **William Marshall**, a twenty-eight-year-old volunteer from Arkansas, served as a rifleman with Captain Blazeby's infantry company. Private Marshall was killed at the Alamo.

■ **Albert Martin**, a twenty-eight-year-old general store owner from Gonzales, Texas, held the rank of captain. He left the Alamo as a courier on February 24, 1836, but returned to the Alamo with the

Gonzales Ranging Company. Captain Martin was killed at the Alamo.

■ **Edward McCafferty**, a volunteer from Refugio, Texas, held the rank of lieutenant. Lieutenant McCafferty was killed at the Alamo.

■ **Jesse McCoy**, a thirty-two-year-old sheriff from Gonzales, Texas, arrived with the Gonzales Ranging Company and served as a rifleman. Private McCoy was killed at the Alamo.

■ **William McDowell**, a forty-three-year-old volunteer from Tennessee, served as a rifleman with Captain Harrison's company. Private McDowell was killed at the Alamo.

■ **James McGee** came to Texas by way of New Orleans as a member of the New Orleans Greys. He served as a rifleman with Captain Blazeby's infantry company. Private McGee was killed at the Alamo.

■ **John McGregor**, a twenty-eight-year-old volunteer from Nacogdoches, Texas, held the rank of 2nd sergeant with Captain Carey's artillery company. Sergeant McGregor was killed at the Alamo.

■ **Robert McKinney**, a twenty-seven-year-old volunteer who came to Texas from New Orleans, served as a rifleman. Private McKinney was killed at the Alamo.

■ **Eliel Melton**, a thirty-eight-year-old merchant from Nashville-on-the-Brazos, Texas, held the rank of lieutenant and served as quartermaster and staff officer. Lieutenant Melton was killed at the Alamo.

■ **Thomas R. Miller**, a forty-one-year-old town clerk, general store owner and farmer from Gonzales, Texas, arrived with the Gonzales Ranging Company and served as a rifleman. Private Miller was killed at the Alamo.

■ **William Mills**, a twenty-one-year-old volunteer from Austin's Colony, Texas, served as rifleman. Private Mills was killed at the Alamo.

■ **Isaac Millsaps**, a forty-one-year-old volunteer from Gonzales, Texas, arrived with the Gonzales Ranging Company and served as a rifleman. Private Millsaps was killed at the Alamo.

■ **Edward F. Mitchasson**, a thirty-year-old doctor from Washington County, Texas, possibly served as surgeon. Private Mitchasson was killed at the Alamo.

■ **Edwin T. Mitchell**, a thirty-year-old volunteer, served as a rifleman with Captain White's infantry company. Private Mitchell was killed at the Alamo.

■ **Napoleon B. Mitchell**, a thirty-two-year-old volunteer, served as an artilleryman with Captain Carey's artillery company. Private Mitchell was killed at the Alamo.

■ **Robert B. Moore**, a fifty-five-year-old volunteer, came to Texas by way of New Orleans with the New Orleans Greys. He served as a rifleman with Captain Blazeby's infantry company. Private Moore was killed at the Alamo.

■ **Willis A. Moore**, a twenty-eight-year-old volunteer from Mississippi, served as a rifleman. Private Moore was killed at the Alamo.

■ **Robert Musselman**, a thirty-one-year-old former United States soldier from Pennsylvania, held the rank of sergeant in Captain Blazeby's infantry company. Sergeant Musselman was killed at the Alamo.

■ **Andres Nava**, a twenty-six-year-old volunteer from San Antonio, Texas, served as a rifleman with Captain Seguín's cavalry company. Private Nava was killed at the Alamo.

■ **George Neggan**, a twenty-eight-year-old volunteer from Gonzales, Texas, arrived with the Gonzales Ranging Company and served as a rifleman. Private Neggan was killed at the Alamo.

■ **Andrew M. Nelson**, a twenty-seven-year-old volunteer, served as a rifleman. Private Nelson was killed at the Alamo.

■ **Edward Nelson**, a twenty-year-old volunteer from South Carolina, served as a rifleman, possibly with Captain Baker's company. Private Nelson was killed at the Alamo.

■ **George Nelson**, a thirty-one-year-old volunteer from South Carolina, served as a rifleman with Captain Blazeby's infantry company. Private Nelson was killed at the Alamo.

■ **Benjamin F. Nobles** held the rank of lieutenant and served as a company officer with Captain Dimmit's company. Lieutenant Nobles left the Alamo on February 26, 1836 with Captain Dimmit to reconnoiter the Mexican army. He did not return to the Alamo.

■ **James Northcross**, a thirty-two-year-old Methodist minister from Bastrop, Texas, served as an artilleryman with Captain Carey's artillery company. Private Northcross was killed at the Alamo.

■ **James Nowlan**, a twenty-seven-year-old volunteer from England, served as a rifleman. Private Nowlan was killed at the Alamo.

■ **William Sanders Oury**, an eighteen-year-old volunteer from Texas, served as a rifleman and courier. Private Oury left the Alamo as a courier on February 29, 1836.

■ **George Pagan** was a twenty-six-year-old volunteer who came to Texas from Natchez, Mississippi. Private Pagan was killed at the Alamo.

■ **Christopher Adams Parker**, a twenty-two-year-old volunteer from Vehlein's Colony, Texas, served as a rifleman. Private Parker was killed at the Alamo.

■ **William Parks**, a thirty-one-year-old volunteer from Austin's Colony, Texas, served as a rifleman with Captain White's infantry company. Private Parks was killed at the Alamo.

■ **William Hester Patton**, a twenty-eight-year-old merchant and surveyor from Brazoria County, Texas, held the rank of captain and commanded a small company. It is believed that Captain Patton left the Alamo as a courier.

■ **Richardson Perry**, a nineteen-year-old volunteer from Brazos County, Texas, served as an artilleryman with Captain Carey's artillery company. Private Perry was killed at the Alamo.

■ **Amos Pollard**, a thirty-two-year-old doctor from Columbia, Texas, held the rank of regimental surgeon and served as chief surgeon and staff officer. Dr. Pollard was killed at the Alamo.

■ **John Purdy Reynolds**, a twenty-nine-year-old doctor from Mifflin County, Pennsylvania, served as a rifleman with Captain Harrison's company. Private Reynolds was killed at the Alamo.

■ **Thomas H. Roberts** served as a rifleman, possibly with Captain Baker's company. Private Roberts was killed at the Alamo.

■ **James Waters Robertson**, a twenty-four-year-old volunteer who came to Texas from Louisiana, served as a rifleman. Private Robertson was killed at the Alamo.

■ **— Robinson**, a twenty-eight-year-old volunteer who came to Texas from Louisiana, held the rank of 4th sergeant in Captain Carey's artillery company. Sergeant Robinson was killed at the Alamo.

■ **James M. Rose**, a thirty-one-year-old volunteer from Arkansas, served as a rifleman. Private Rose was killed at the Alamo.

■ **Louis Rose**, a fifty-year-old former French soldier, sawmill worker and teamster from Nacogdoches, Texas, served as a rifleman. Private Rose left the Alamo sometime between March 3 and March 6, 1836.

■ **Jackson J. Rusk**, a volunteer from Nacogdoches, Texas, served as a rifleman. Private Rusk was killed at the Alamo.

■ **Joseph Rutherford**, a thirty-eight-year-old volunteer from Nacogdoches, Texas, served as an artilleryman with Captain Carey's artillery company. Private Rutherford was killed at the Alamo.

■ **Isaac Ryan**, a thirty-one-year-old volunteer from Louisiana, served as a rifleman with Captain White's infantry company. Private Ryan was killed at the Alamo.

■ **Mial Scurlock**, a twenty-seven-year-old volunteer from San Augustine, Texas, served as a rifleman. Private Scurlock was killed at the Alamo.

■ **Juan Neopmuceno Seguín**, a twenty-nine-year-old rancher and political chief of San Antonio, Texas, held the rank of captain and was the commanding officer of a cavalry company. Captain Seguín left the Alamo on February 25, 1836 as a courier to rally reinforcements. The Alamo fell before Seguín was able to return.

■ **Marcus L. Sewell**, a thirty-one-year-old shoemaker from Gonzales, Texas, served as a rifleman with the Gonzales Ranging Company. Private Sewell was killed at the Alamo.

■ **Manson Shied**, a twenty-five-year-old carpenter from Brazoria, Texas, served as an artilleryman with Captain Carey's artillery company. Private Shied was killed at the Alamo.

■ **Cleveland Kinloch Simmons**, a twenty-year-old volunteer from South Carolina, held the rank of 1st lieutenant and served as a company officer in Captain Forsyth's cavalry company. Lieutenant Simmons was killed at the Alamo.

■ **Andrew H. Smith**, a twenty-one-year-old volunteer who came to Texas from Tennessee, served as a rifleman. It is believed that Private Smith was killed at the Alamo.

■ **Charles S. Smith,** a thirty-year-old volunteer who came to Texas from Louisiana, served as an artilleryman with Captain Carey's artillery company. Private Smith was killed at the Alamo.

■ **John William Smith**, a forty-four-year-old civil engineer, carpenter and boardinghouse keeper from San Antonio, Texas, served as a scout, courier and guide. On February 23, 1836, he left the Alamo as a courier. He returned on March 1, 1836 as the scout and guide for the Gonzales Ranging Company. He left again on March 3, 1836 carrying some of the last letters and communications. He was on his way back with twenty-five volunteers when the Alamo fell.

■ **Joshua G. Smith**, a twenty-eight-year-old volunteer from Bastrop, Texas, held the rank of sergeant in Captain Forsyth's cavalry company. Sergeant Smith was killed at the Alamo.

■ **William H. Smith**, a twenty-five-year-old volunteer from Nacogdoches, Texas, served as an artilleryman with Captain Carey's artillery company. Private Smith was killed at the Alamo.

■ **Launcelot Smither**, a thirty-six-year-old horse trader, farmer, and medic from Austin's Colony, Texas, served as a courier.

Private Smither left the Alamo on February 23, 1836, possibly as a courier.

■ **Andrew Jackson Sowell**, a twenty-year-old farmer from Gonzales, Texas, served as a rifleman and courier. Private Sowell left the Alamo as a courier.

■ **Richard Starr**, a twenty-five-year-old resident of England, came to Texas by way of New Orleans with the New Orleans Greys. He served as a rifleman with Captain Blazeby's infantry company. Private Starr was killed at the Alamo.

■ **James E. Stewart**, a twenty-eight-year-old volunteer, served as a rifleman. Private Stewart was killed at the Alamo.

■ **Richard L. Stockton**, a nineteen-year-old volunteer from Virginia, served as a rifleman with Captain Harrison's company. Private Stockton was killed at the Alamo.

■ **A. Spain Summerlin**, a nineteen-year-old volunteer from San Augustine, Texas, served as a rifleman with Captain White's infantry company. Private Summerlin was killed at the Alamo.

■ **William E. Summers**, a twenty-four-year-old volunteer from Gonzales, Texas, arrived with the Gonzales Ranging Company and served as a rifleman. Private Summers was killed at the Alamo.

■ **John Sutherland**, a forty-three-year-old doctor from Tuscumbia, Alabama, served as a medical assistant, scout, and courier with Captain Patton's Company. Private Sutherland left the Alamo as a courier on February 23, 1836. The Alamo fell before he was able to return.

■ **William dePriest Sutherland**, a seventeen-year-old medical student from Navidad, Texas, served as a rifleman. Private Sutherland was killed at the Alamo.

■ **Edward Taylor**, a twenty-four-year-old farm hand from Liberty, Texas, served as a rifleman. His brothers, George and James, were with him at the Alamo. Private Taylor was killed at the Alamo.

■ **George Taylor**, a twenty-year-old farm hand from Liberty, Texas, served as a rifleman. Private Taylor was killed at the Alamo.

■ **James Taylor**, a twenty-two-year-old farm hand from Liberty, Texas, served as a rifleman. Private Taylor was killed at the Alamo.

■ **William Taylor**, a thirty-seven-year-old volunteer from Little River Community, Texas, served as a rifleman. Private Taylor was killed at the Alamo.

■ **B. Archer M. Thomas**, an eighteen-year-old volunteer from Logan County, Kentucky, served as a rifleman with Captain Harrison's company. Private Thomas was killed at the Alamo.

■ **Henry Thomas**, a twenty-five-year-old volunteer from Germany who had come to Texas by way of New Orleans with the New Orleans Greys, served as a rifleman with Captain Blazeby's infantry company. Private Thomas was killed at the Alamo.

■ **Jesse G. Thompson**, a thirty-eight-year-old volunteer from Brazoria, Texas, served as a rifleman. Private Thompson was killed at the Alamo.

■ **John W. Thomson**, a twenty-nine-year-old doctor from Tennessee, served as a rifleman and possibly a surgeon. Private Thomson was killed at the Alamo.

■ **John M. Thurston**, a twenty-three-year-old volunteer who came to Texas from Kentucky, held the rank of 2nd lieutenant. He was a company officer in Captain Forsyth's cavalry company. Lieutenant Thurston was killed at the Alamo.

■ **Burke Trammel**, a twenty-six-year-old volunteer from Tennessee, served as an artilleryman with Captain Carey's artillery company. Private Trammel was killed at the Alamo.

■ **William Barret Travis**, a twenty-six-year-old lawyer, newspaperman, and teacher from San Felipe, Texas, held the rank of lieutenant colonel and was the commanding officer of the Alamo garrison. Lieutenant Colonel Travis was killed at the Alamo with a shot through the forehead. He may have been the first to die.

■ **George W. Tumlinson**, a twenty-two-year-old volunteer from Gonzales, Texas, arrived with the Gonzales Ranging Company and served as an artilleryman with Captain Carey's artillery company. Private Tumlinson was killed at the Alamo.

■ **James Tylee**, a forty-one-year-old volunteer from Texas, served as a rifleman. Private Tylee was killed at the Alamo.

■ **Asa Walker**, a twenty-three-year-old volunteer from Tennessee, served as a rifleman with Captain White's infantry company. Private Walker was killed at the Alamo.

■ **Jacob Walker**, a thirty-seven-year-old volunteer from Nacogdoches, Texas, served as an artilleryman with Captain Carey's artillery company. Private Walker was killed at the Alamo.

■ **William B. Ward**, a thirty-year-old volunteer who came to Texas from New Orleans, held the rank of sergeant. Sergeant Ward was killed at the Alamo.

■ **Henry Warnell**, a twenty-four-year-old jockey and hunter from Bastrop, Texas, served as an artilleryman with Captain Carey's artillery company. Private Warnell escaped from the Alamo on March 6, 1836 and died of his wounds two months later.

■ **Joseph G. Washington**, a twenty-eight-year-old volunteer, served as a rifleman with Captain Harrison's company. Private Washington was killed at the Alamo.

■ **Thomas Waters**, a twenty-four-year-old volunteer from England who came to Texas by way of New Orleans with the New Orleans Greys, served as an artilleryman with Captain Carey's artillery company. Private Waters was killed at the Alamo.

■ **William Wells**, a thirty-seven-year-old volunteer from Georgia, served as a rifleman. Private Wells was killed at the Alamo.

■ **Isaac White** was either from Alabama or Kentucky and held the rank of sergeant. Sergeant White was killed at the Alamo.

■ **Robert White**, a thirty-year-old from Gonzales, Texas, arrived with the Gonzales Ranging Company. He held the rank of captain and was a commanding officer of an infantry company. Captain White was killed at the Alamo.

■ **Hiram James Williamson**, a twenty-six-year-old volunteer from Washington-on-the- Brazos, Texas, held the rank of sergeant major. He was the ranking NCO of the Alamo garrison staff. Sergeant Major Williamson was killed at the Alamo.

■ **William Wills**, a farmer from Brazoria County, Texas, served as a rifleman. Private Wills was killed at the Alamo.

■ **David L. Wilson**, a twenty-nine-year-old volunteer from Nacogdoches, Texas, served as a rifleman. Private Wilson was killed at the Alamo.

■ **John Wilson**, a thirty-two-year-old volunteer, served as a rifleman. Private Wilson was killed at the Alamo.

■ **Anthony Wolf**, a fifty-four-year-old volunteer from Washington County, Texas, had served as an infantry lieutenant in the Louisiana Territorial Militia in 1806. He served at the Alamo as an artilleryman with Captain Carey's artillery company. Private Wolf was killed at the Alamo.

■ **Claiborne Wright**, a twenty-six-year-old volunteer from Gonzales, Texas, arrived with the Gonzales Ranging Company and served as a rifleman. Private Wright was killed at the Alamo.

■ **Damacio Ximenes**, a volunteer from Texas, served as a rifleman. Private Ximenes was killed at the Alamo.

■ **Charles Zanco**, a twenty-eight-year-old painter and farmer from Harris County, Texas, held the rank of lieutenant. He served as assistant to the ordnance chief, Ordnance Department. Lieutenant Zanco was killed at the Alamo.

Chapter Ten

Victory or Death

Words and Deeds of Bravery and Courage

Besieged by Santa Anna and desperately short of men and ammunition, Colonel Travis knew the survival of the Alamo garrison depended on how quickly Texians rallied to their aid. Although Travis dispatched a number of impassioned pleas for help, only thirty-two men arrived in time to lend assistance. By the time Travis' famous letter of February 24, 1836 reached the United States, he and his men were already dead. Travis' message and subsequent news of the fall of the Alamo brought hundreds of volunteers from all over the country determined to avenge the deaths of the Alamo defenders.

Tradition has it that sixteen couriers were sent out from the Alamo. Some claim the number may be as high as twenty. Dr. Sutherland and John Smith were the first two couriers to leave the mission; young James Allen was the last. It is believed that four couriers risked their lives to return to the Alamo: John Smith, Albert Martin, Charles Despallier, and James Bonham.

■ Travis' letters contain significant information on the Texas side of the Alamo story, and reveal the bravery and courage of William Barret Travis. His February 23, 1836 letter to Colonel Fannin in Goliad reads as follows:

"We have removed all our men into the Alamo. . . .We have one hundred and forty-six men, who are determined never to retreat. We have little provisions, but enough to serve us till you and your men arrive. We deem it unnecessary to repeat to a brave officer, who knows his duty, that we call on him for assistance. . ."

■ Travis sent John Smith to deliver this message.

■ Travis wrote another letter on February 23, 1836 "To Any of the inhabitants of Texas":

"The enemy in large force is in sight. We want men and provisions. Send them to us. We have 150 men and are determined to defend the Alamo to the last. Give us assistance."

The message was originally addressed to "Andrew Ponton, Judge, Gonzales." Travis crossed it out and wrote instead, "To any of the inhabitants of Texas." Dr. Sutherland rode out of the Alamo with the dispatch.

■ The next day, February 24, Travis penned another dispatch, this one "To the People of Texas & All Americans in the world." It is considered by many as one of the masterpieces of American patriotism:

"Fellow Citizens & Compatriots—I am besieged by a thousand or more of the Mexicans under Santa Anna—The enemy has demanded surrender at discretion, otherwise the garrison are to be put to the sword, if the fort is taken—I have answered the demand with cannon shot, & our flag still waves proudly from the walls—I shall never surrender or retreat. Then, I call on you in the name of Liberty, of patriotism & every thing dear to the American character, to come to our aid with all dispatch—The enemy is receiving reinforcements daily & will no doubt increase to three of four thousand in four or five days. If this call is neglected, I am determined to sustain myself as long as possible & die like a soldier who never forgets what is due to his own honor & that of his country—Victory or Death!"

■ Albert Martin was chosen to deliver this message to the nearest town of Gonzales, about seventy miles away. Martin added his own message on the back: "Hurry on all the men you can."

■ Launcelot Smithers took the message from Martin in Gonzales and rode ninety miles to San Felipe to deliver the news. Smithers added his own postscript to the dispatch: "I hope that Every one will Randeves at Gonzales as soon poseble as the Brave Soldiers are suffering. do not neglect the powder. is very scarce and should not be delad one moment."

■ Fearing a major assault, Travis sent an urgent appeal to San Houston on February 25, 1836: "I shall hold out to the last extremity. If they overpower us, we shall fall a sacrifice at the shrine of our country, and we hope posterity and our country will do our memory justice. Give me help, oh my Country! Victory or Death!"

■ Travis and his men believed that the garrison was completely surrounded and no one was anxious to carry Travis' message to Houston. The men initially elected Juan Seguín, but Travis objected since he needed Seguín to stay with the garrison. Seguín spoke fluent Spanish and knew the customs of the Mexicans outside the fort as well as the Tejanos inside. The men insisted, however, and Seguín left with the message that night.

■ On March 3, 1836, Travis wrote a letter to his friend David Ayres Montville. Travis tore a strip from some old yellow wrapping paper and quickly dashed off a personal request: "Take care of my little boy. If the country should be saved, I may make for him a splendid fortune; but if the country be lost and I should perish, he will have nothing but the proud recollection that he is the son of a man who died for his country."

■ On that same day, Travis sent another dispatch to his friend Jesse Grimes explaining why he was making his stand at the Alamo. "Let the Convention go on and make a declaration of independence, and we will then understand, and the world will understand, what we are fighting for," Travis wrote. "If independence is not declared, I shall lay down my arms, and so will the men under my command. But under the flag of independence, we are ready to peril our lives a hundred times a day."

■ Tragically, Travis never learned that Independence had been declared on March 2, 1836, just one day before he wrote his letter to Grimes.

Responses to Travis' calls for reinforcements

■ Governor Smith read Travis' appeal "To the People of Texas & all the world," and called on the colonists in San Felipe "to fly to the aid of your besieged countrymen and not permit them to be massacred by a mercenary foe. I slight none! The call is upon ALL who are able to bear arms, to rally without one moment's delay, or in fifteen days the heart of Texas will be the seat of war." Colonel Sidney Sherman and his band of fifty-two mercenaries from Kentucky heard the call and prepared to march for the Alamo.

Bonham returns

■ James Bonham returned to the Alamo for the second time on March 3. Determined to deliver his message at any cost, he rode between two enemy positions, making it through without the Mexicans firing a shot. He brought a letter from Three-Legged Willie Williamson that claimed sixty volunteers were on their way from San Felipe. In addition, Williamson told Travis that Fannin was at last on the march with 300 men and a battery of four cannon. At least 300 more volunteers were due to reach San Felipe and would be sent on their way as quickly as possible. "For God's sake hold out until we can assist you," Williamson pleaded.

■ Many historians claim than Bonham arrived on March 3 with a message that Fannin was not sending reinforcements. In Travis' letter to the Convention on the same day, he acknowledged Bonham's return to the compound that morning and also wrote: "Colonel Fannin is said to be on the march to this place with reinforcements; but I fear it is not true, as I have repeatedly sent to him for aid without receiving any."

Aid from Gonzales

■ The only aid that Travis received was from the Gonzales Ranging Company. In response to Travis' call for help, twenty-five men from the Gonzales Ranging Company headed out for the Alamo on February 27. Lieutenant George Kimball led the group with Albert Martin by his side. Martin was the courier who had delivered Travis' message of February 24 to Gonzales. John Smith, who knew the country better than anyone, served as their guide.

■ As the Gonzales Ranging Company rode out of town, they passed by John C. King's place. His young son, William P. King, ran out and begged to go in place of his father. He was needed at home with nine children to feed and William felt he could serve just as well. The switch was made and they continued on.

■ The Gonzales men stopped at Cibolo on February 28 looking for new recruits. They picked up seven more men. They rested most of February 29 and the thirty-two men left Cibolo at sunset in order to arrive at the Alamo in the dark of night.

■ The Gonzales Ranging Company approached the Alamo under cover of nightfall on March 1. When they were close enough to see the fort, a sentry fired and hit one of the Gonzales men in the foot. The rest called out for the sentry to stop shooting. The firing stopped and the gate swung open to welcome the long-awaited reinforcements. The spirits of the defenders must have fallen when they saw there were only thirty-two men riding in to assist them. All thirty-two died in the Alamo. A monument was erected at Gonzales to honor their sacrifice.

The Immortal Thirty-Two:

Issac G. Baker	Thomas Jackson
John Cane	Johnnie Kellog
George W. Cottle	Andrew Kent
David P. Cummings	George C. Kimball
Jacob C. Darst	William P. King
John Davis	Jonathan L. Lindley
Squire Daymon	Albert Martin
William Dearduff	Jesse McCoy
Charles Despallier	Thomas R. Miller
William Fishbaugh	Isaac Millsaps
John Flanders	George Neggan
Dolphin Ward Floyd	John W. Smith
Galba Fuqua	William E. Summers
John E. Garvin	George W. Tumlinson
John E. Gaston	Robert White
James George	Claiborne Wright

Courageous deeds were not limited to couriers and the men from Gonzales. . .

■ According to Susannah Dickenson, 16-year-old Galba Fuqua, ran into the baptistery during the Alamo battle. A lead ball had shattered his jaw and he was unable to speak. He held together the broken parts of his jaw and tried again. Still unable to speak, he shook his head in despair and returned to the fight.

■ Susannah's husband ran into the baptistery. "Great God, Sue," the artillery captain said, "the Mexicans are inside our walls! All is lost! If they spare you, save my child." He gave Susannah a parting kiss, then drew his sword and returned to battle.

■ After the Mexicans entered the Alamo compound, a Mexican soldier demanded Gertrudis Navarro hand over her money and her husband. She told him she had neither. Just then a sick rebel appeared at Juana's side and tried to defend her from the soldiers, but he was immediately bayoneted by the Mexicans.

■ Walter Lane, a 19-year-old soldier, found himself in the midst of Mexican cavalrymen following the first engagement at San Jacinto on April 20. One of the cavalrymen caught Lane in the shoulder and knocked him from his horse. The fall knocked him unconscious, but he rose to his feet a few minutes later and staggered toward friendly lines. The Mexicans saw him and several lancers bore down on him. As they were about to impale the boy, Mirabeau Lamar blocked their path and shot one of the Mexicans. Henry Karnes galloped in, pulled Lane up behind him and carried him to safety. The Mexicans dragoons reportedly applauded as the three Texians rode for cover. Lamar turned toward his adversaries and made a gracious bow.

Nor were courageous deeds limited to the Texians. . .

■ A number of Mexican soldiers who had gained entry to the Alamo plaza noticed a rebel flag hanging from a pole atop the Long Barracks. Three of the Zapadores ran at the objective. All three fell, cut down by gunfire. A sub-lieutenant of the same corps, José Maria Torres, climbed to the top of the barracks and pulled the flag down. Torres raised the tricolor of the Zapadores just before he was shot and mortally wounded.

■ Colonel Francisco Duque, Toluca Battalion commander, was hit in the thigh by shrapnel from an artillery blast during the battle of the Alamo. He fell to the ground and was trampled by his own men, but continued to cheer them on until his subordinate took over command.

■ General Manuel Fernandez Castrillón met a heroic death at San Jacinto directing a gun crew during the battle. Most of his artillerymen were killed and the others ran away, calling for the General to come with them. He refused. "I have been in 40 battles and never showed my back," Castrillión answered calmly. "I am too old to do it now." He turned to face the enemy.

Chapter Eleven

The Battle of the Alamo

The Alamo Siege (February 23 – March 5, 1836)

General Santa Anna arrived in San Antonio on February 23, 1836 and began a 12-day siege of the Alamo. Colonel Travis knew he desperately needed reinforcements in order to hold the garrison, and sent out message after message calling for men and supplies. The Alamo defenders spent their final days fortifying the garrison while the Mexican soldiers dug a series of entrenchments closer and closer to the Alamo walls each night.

Day One—February 23, 1836:

■ The first to see the arrival of the Mexican troops was a soldier posted in the belfry of the San Fernando Church in San Antonio de Béxar. He began ringing the church bell and yelled, "The enemy is in view." Lieutenant Colonel William Barret Travis and a group of soldiers climbed to the top of the belfry but could see no sign of troops.

■ Dr. John Sutherland, and John "El Coronado" Smith rode out to see if they could see any sign of the enemy. A mile and a half outside of town, they came face to face with several hundred Mexican cavalry. Sutherland and Smith turned around and headed back to town.

■ Travis ordered an immediate evacuation of the town. The entire rebel garrison made preparations to take position inside the fortress.

■ The Mexican cavalrymen began their descent from the Alazan hills in full view of the town. From the time the first Mexican troopers entered the town, more than an hour elapsed before they were present in full strength. Santa Anna entered San Antonio de Béxar unopposed and the town quietly switched hands. Not a single shot had been fired.

■ Travis watched as the head of the Mexican column arrived. In an act of defiance, he ordered a flag raised from a makeshift staff. Perhaps it was the flag he bought in San Felipe for five dollars (of which no reliable description remains). The Mexicans believed it was the national tricolor, with two stars in the middle denoting the two states of Coahuila and Texas. This certainly was not the case, for Travis and his men were fighting for independence.

■ Captain Almeron Dickenson rode into town to rescue his wife Susannah and their infant daughter, Angelina. As the Mexican troops began to appear on the streets, Captain Dickenson picked up his family and headed for the southern entrance of the Alamo.

■ If the Dolores Cavalry Regiment had pursued Sutherland and Smith closely, they would have caught many of the garrison still running through the streets. Santa Anna would later claim that if his cavalrymen had not dawdled that morning, he would have taken the Alamo without a fight.

■ David Crockett asked Travis where he and his Tennesseans should post themselves. Most accounts claim that Travis placed Crockett and his skilled rifleman at what seemed the weakest link in the fort's defensive perimeter: the low picket barricade between the chapel and the south wall.

■ Travis wrote one of his first messages to Colonel Fannin in Goliad. "We have removed all our men into the Alamo. . . .We have one hundred and forty-six men, who are determined never to retreat. We have little provisions, but enough to serve us till you and your men arrive. We deem it unnecessary to repeat to a brave officer, who knows his duty, that we shall call on him for assistance."

■ The next message was to be delivered to Gonzales. "The enemy in large force is in sight. We want men and provisions. Send them to us. We have 150 men and are determined to defend the Alamo to the last. Give us assistance." Dr. Sutherland rode out of the Alamo with the dispatch.

■ A "blood red" flag was raised by the Mexicans on the Alamo side of the San Fernando Church belfry soon after they occupied the town. It was plainly visible and signified no mercy. Santa Anna told his staff repeatedly in San Antonio, "I neither ask nor give quarter."

■ In response to the crimson flag, Travis ordered his 18-pounder cannon fired. The Mexicans unlimbered their cannon and sent four shells into the Alamo compound; none did any harm.

Attempts to Parley

■ Colonel James Bowie wanted to try a parley with Santa Anna. Although Travis disagreed, Bowie went ahead on his own. He seized the first paper in sight, a blank page from a child's copybook, and dictated a note to Juan Seguín. Bowie looked at the note and saw that Seguín had signed it with the standard, "God and the Mexican Federation." Bowie crossed it out and wrote instead, "God and Texas."

■ Green Jameson, the Alamo's engineer, carried James Bowie's message under a flag of truce. Jameson returned with a message from Santa Anna refusing to discuss terms with "rebel-

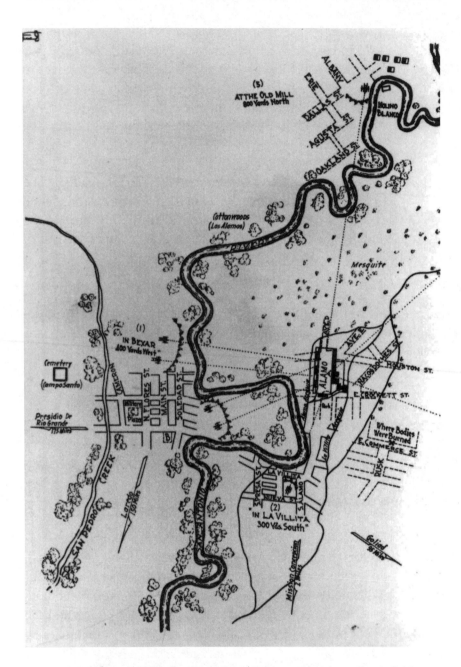

Siege of the Alamo 1836. San Antonio de Béxar—the Alamo Battlefield.
Texas State Library & Archives Commission.

lious foreigners to whom there is no other recourse left, if they wish to save their lives, than to place themselves immediately at the disposal of the Supreme Government." Travis interpreted this as a surrender "at discretion."

■ Travis sent a verbal message by his own man, Albert Martin, to Colonel Juan Almonte of Santa Anna's staff. If Almonte wished to talk to Travis, he would be glad to open discussion. Almonte sent word that it was not his place to speak on behalf of Santa Anna and reiterated the General's conditional offer. Travis told Martin to tell Almonte that he would let him know if he accepted their terms. Otherwise, he would fire another round from his cannon.

■ Travis assembled the men to inform them of the enemy's terms. The garrison pledged to never surrender. Travis immediately ordered the gunners to send his reply with a cannon. They would stand and fight.

Day Two— February 24:

■ Santa Anna ordered his men to maintain a continuous fire on the Alamo while trying to prevent any possible movement of men or supplies into or out of the mission. None of his cannon were powerful enough to seriously damage the Alamo's thick stone and adobe walls immediately. Santa Anna's 12-pounder artillery pieces were still far to the south.

■ Lacking heavy ordnance, the Mexican gunners had to place their smaller cannon closer to the walls, but the Texian rifleman made it dangerous to come within 200 yards of the Alamo in daylight. Forced to work after dark, the Mexican soldiers began to dig a series of entrenchments and approached the compound in this manner.

■ Although tightly blockaded, the Alamo was not completely sealed off by the Mexican army. Non-combatants occasionally went in and out during the night and Travis was able to dispatch couriers in various directions appealing for reinforcements.

■ Texian riflemen were still a threat at night. Late on February 24, a Texian saw Colonel Juan Bringas crossing the foot-bridge leading across the river with five or six men on a scouting mission. The Texians opened fire. One Mexican was killed and the rest ran back across the bridge.

■ Bowie, who had been ill for some time, became dramatically worse on February 24. Believing he was contagious, he insisted on leaving his sister-in-law's quarters rather than endanger her and her child and sister. He summoned two soldiers to come and help him away. Before he left he tried to comfort Juana. "Sister, do not be afraid," he told her. "I leave you with Colonel Travis, Colonel Crockett, and other friends, and [they] will treat you kindly." He made his way to a small room immediately left of the main gate, next to the officer's quarters.

■ Incapacitated by the illness, Bowie relinquished command and instructed his volunteers to obey Travis. Travis was now in full command of the garrison; thereafter he signed every dispatch after February 24 as the commanding colonel.

■ Travis wrote the most famous of his messages on February 24, addressed "To the People of Texas & all Americans in the world." (See *Victory or Death*)

Day Three—February 25:

■ Many people do not realize that whenever possible, Travis and his men resorted to offensive tactics to stall enemy advances.

■ Two hundred or more Mexicans crossed the river on the morning of February 25 under cover of some houses near the southwest corner of the fort. The defenders opened a heavy discharge of grape and canister, together with a well directed fire from small arms, which forced the Mexicans to take shelter in the small houses 90 to 100 yards from their batteries. The fighting continued for about two hours until the enemy withdrew in confusion. Travis saw them carry off about eight more dead and wounded. None of the defenders were hit.

■ Robert Brown, Charles Despallier, James Rose and several others ran out of the Alamo gate in the face of enemy fire and set fire to houses, which had given the enemy shelter. This gave the Texians a better field of fire and the Mexicans lost their best cover.

■ Fearing an eminent Mexican assault, Travis sent an urgent appeal to Sam Houston. "I shall hold out to the last extremity. If they overpower us, we shall fall a sacrifice at the shrine of our country, and we hope posterity and our country will do our memory justice. Give my help, oh my Country! Victory or death!"

■ The Mexicans moved in closer on the night of February 25. Colonel Juan Morales led a detachment to dig trenches covering the ground in La Villita, a jumble of shacks and huts, dangerously close to the Alamo. Two new batteries were also planted. One was placed about 300 yards south of the Alamo and the other was placed near the powder house, which was one thousand yards to the southeast. The Matamoros battalion moved up to support both.

Day Four—February 26:

■ A new threat appeared at first light when the Texians discovered a detachment of General Ramírez y Sesma's cavalry circling toward the river of the Alamo. A group of Texians raced out the northern gate to meet them head-on and was able to drive the Mexicans back with rifle fire.

■ In an effort to fortify their defenses, Green Jameson's men dug more trenches and more earthworks to strengthen the walls and serve as parapets. They were under constant fire. Sesma's eight guns were now to the west, southwest, and southeast.

■ The deadly riflemen in the Alamo kept a constant watch for Mexicans careless enough to show their heads. The Texians used the nearby irrigation ditches and Jameson's earthen parapets for cover. The Mexicans soon learned to keep down.

■ While a constant cannonade poured forth from Santa Anna's batteries, the Alamo's guns fired only occasionally. Ammunition was low and could not be wasted. Fortunately, many of the Mexican guns were of the same caliber as the garrison's guns, and solid shot that landed inside the parade ground could be picked up and fired back.

Day Five—February 27:

■ The Alamo defenders discovered Mexican troops by the mill to the north were blocking the irrigation ditch in an effort to cut off the fort's water. Green Jameson put men to work on a half-finished well at the south end of the plaza. They hit water but they also weakened an earth and timber parapet by the low barracks. The mound collapsed and left no way to fire safely over the wall.

■ David Crockett fired on the enemy as Mexican artillerymen set up and operated a forward battery in the bend of the San Antonio River, which angled near the fort. The townspeople were convinced that he killed the very first *soldado* to fall, with a 200-yard shot from his long rifle.

■ Santa Anna rode forward to one of his batteries on the afternoon of February 27, and Texians from the Alamo fired on the Mexican general. The Tejanos in San Antonio swore that one of the bullets that sent Santa Anna rushing back to safety came from Crockett's rifle.

■   Santa Anna sent a message to Mexico City with a report of his success. He described the capture of San Antonio but made no mention of the defiant Texians still held out in the Alamo.

■   Travis wrote another impassioned plea to Fannin and stressed the urgent need for reinforcements. Travis handed the message to James Butler Bonham. Bonham had already delivered one message to Fannin and had returned to the Alamo after the siege began.

Day Six—February 28:

■   Mexican soldiers made another attempt to cut off the garrison's water while a second detachment planted a new battery by the old mill about 800 hundred yards to the north.

■   Santa Anna continued his use of psychological warfare to harass the Texians and break them down. Every night was filled with bugle calls, cheers, volleys of musketry, and bursts of artillery.

Day Seven—February 29:

■   A message from Santa Anna arrived in the compound. The general offered amnesty to any Tejanos in the fort who came out and made no further resistance. The Mexican commander gave them three days to decide.

■   Learning of Santa Anna's offer of amnesty, several Tejanos came to Bowie for advice. The Tejanos were not soldiers and none of them had enlisted or taken oaths. Most had families in San Antonio. "All of you who desire to leave here may go in safety," he told them from his cot. Travis approved as well. In the next few hours several of them left the garrison.

■   When word reached Santa Anna that Colonel Fannin was coming to the Alamo's rescue, the general ordered General Sesma to take the Allende battalion from the east and the Dolores cavalry from the Gonzales road and head down the river toward Goliad. Santa Anna closed his instructions with a final reminder: "In this war, you know, there ought to be no prisoners."

Day Eight—March 1:

■ The only reinforcements the garrison received were thirty-two men from the Gonzales Ranging Company. They approached the Alamo under cover of nightfall on March 1. When they were close enough to see the fort, a Texian sentry fired and hit one the Gonzales men in the foot. Once the firing stopped, the men entered the mission.

■ To honor the new arrivals, Travis allowed the gunners two precious shots to let Santa Anna know they had not forgotten him. With ammunition in short supply, the men sighted carefully. The first ball crashed into the town's Military Plaza. The second tore through the roof of an adjoining house. The gunners had no way of knowing it, but the building served as Santa Anna's headquarters.

Day Nine—March 2:

■ Texas independence was declared at Washington-on-the-Brazos. The Alamo garrison never learned of this historic event.

Day Ten —March 3:

■ At great personal risk, James Bonham returned to the Alamo at 11:00 a.m. He rode between enemy positions and made it through without the Mexicans firing a shot. He brought a letter from Three-Legged Willie Williamson, which claimed that sixty volunteers were on their way from San Felipe. In addition, Williamson told Travis that Fannin was on the march with 300 men and a battery of four cannon. At least three hundred more volunteers would follow. "For God's sake hold out until we can assist you," Williamson pleaded.

■ Travis wrote a series of messages from within the confines of the Alamo, most pleading for assistance that never arrived.

■ Travis wrote another appeal for help to the President of the Convention and gave that message along with two personal letters to John "El Colorado" Smith to deliver. Travis told Smith he would fire the 18-pounder three times a day, once each at morning, noon, and night. Any Texian hearing that gun would know that the men in the Alamo still held out.

■ Mexican entrenchments surrounded the fort. To use Travis' own estimates, "in Béxar (San Antonio), four hundred yards west; in La Villita, three hundred yards south; at the powder house, one thousand yards east of south; on the ditch, eight hundred yards northeast, and at the old mill, eight hundred yards north."

Day Eleven—March 4:

■ At dawn, a new Mexican battery north of the Alamo burst into action. The guns were about 250 yards away and every shot smashed the fort's north wall, showering the plaza with earth and stones. Jameson worked frantically to strengthen the defenses, piling up more dirt against the wall and hammering extra bracing into place.

■ Texians heard the sound of distant cheering. General Gaona's men had finally arrived with the reinforcements Santa Anna had been expecting. The new arrivals would bring the Mexican strength before the Alamo to some 2,500 men and nine pieces of artillery. By this time, Santa Anna outnumbered the Texian defenders more than twelve to one.

■ More good news arrived for the Mexicans. A messenger rode into town and announced General Urrea's victory at San

Patricio. The Mexicans were jubilant. The bells of San Fernando rang out the good news and another red banner was raised on Powder House Hill to the east.

Day Twelve—March 5:

■ The defenders discovered that the Mexican battery on the north had been pushed closer and was now only about 200 yards from the fort. At that range, each shot pounded the adobe wall until a portion collapsed. Jameson directed work parties to reinforce the wall with pieces of timber and anything else they could find. These were only temporary measures, however, and Jameson knew the north wall could not hold out if the Mexican guns continued to fire upon it.

■ Mexican firing tapered off in the late afternoon, and Travis took advantage of the lull to assemble the garrison. According to legend, he drew a line in the dust with his saber and invited all those resolved to stay and die with him to cross over it. Although many historians believe the story is nothing but a myth, Travis did in fact address his men that day. Mrs. Dickenson remembered that he "asked the command that if any desired to escape, now was the time to let it be known, and to step out of ranks." Whether he actually drew a line in the sand, however, is unknown.

■ Travis spent his last night writing another letter and making a will. He returned to his quarters around 4:00 a.m.

Santa Anna Plans the Attack

■ After his reinforcements arrived, Santa Anna called a staff meeting on March 4 and proposed an immediate assault. Several of the officers argued that they were not yet ready for a general assault and wanted to wait until additional artillery arrived.

■ The subject of prisoners was brought up by several senior officers during the staff conference. Some asked that a show of mercy be made. Santa Anna, however, would not be swayed.

■ Despite their objections, he insisted on attacking. He cited morale as a factor, claiming that "an assault would infuse our soldiers with that enthusiasm of the first triumph that would make them superior in the future to those of the enemy."

■ Lieutenant Colonel de la Peña later claimed that Santa Anna feared the enemy garrison was about to surrender. According to de la Peña, "It was for this reason that he precipitated the assault, because he wanted to cause a sensation and would have regretted taking the Alamo without clamor and without bloodshed, for some believed that without these there is no glory."

■ De la Peña recorded that the majority of officers "were of the opinion that victory over a handful of men concentrated in the Alamo did not call for a great sacrifice." He claimed that most men were horrified at Santa Anna's decision but "chose silence, knowing that he would not tolerate opposition."

■ Captain José Juan Sánchez-Navarro wrote in his diary, "Why is it that Santa Anna always wants to mark his triumphs with blood and tears?"

■ Santa Anna spent March 4 and 5 planning his attack. His orders for the assault were issued at 2:00 p.m. on March 5 and displayed his talent for careful and meticulous preparation. The attack was set for the early morning of Sunday, March 6.

■ All recruits and untrained volunteers, perhaps 400 men, were to remain in camp. Only seasoned men were to be used in the assault.

The formations and objectives of the various Mexican assaulting columns were as follows:

■   General Cós led the first column, and if he fell, Santa Anna himself would take over the column. The first column consisted of three hundred men drawn from the Aldama and San Luis battalions. They were to carry ten ladders, two crowbars, and two axes. Their objective was the west wall.

■   The second column was commanded by Colonel Frances Duque. If Colonel Duque fell, General Manuel Castrillión would take command. The second column was composed of four hundred men from the Toluca and San Luis battalions. They were to carry ten ladders, two crowbars, and two axes. Their objective was the north wall.

■   Colonel José Maria Romero headed up the third assault column. If Colonel Romero fell, command would pass to Colonel Mariano de Salas. The third column consisted of four hundred men drawn from the Matamoros, Jiménez, and San Luis battalions. They carried six ladders. Their objective was the east wall.

■   Colonel Juan Morales would command the fourth and smallest column. If Colonel Morales fell, Colonel José Miñon would take command. The fourth column was composed of about one hundred men from the Matamoros, Jiménez, and San Luis battalions. They carried only two ladders. Their objective was the south gate and the wooden-stake palisade that ran diagonally from the chapel to the south wall.

■   There was a fifth reserve column under the command of Colonel Amat. This final assaulting block was made up of the elite Zapadores (corps of engineers) plus five companies of *grenadiers* (heavy infantry), about four hundred men in all. They would be posted at the Mexican's north battery.

■   There were 300 men in the cavalry force under General Sesma. It would be their responsibility to scout the countryside during the battle and to prevent any attempts at escape by the enemy—or their own men.

Preparation for Battle

■ At sunset on March 5, the Mexican beehive of activity paused, and the north battery ceased fire.

■ **5:00 p.m.** The *grenadiers* headed through town and up stream to join the Zapadores battalion at the reserves' assembly point.

■ **7:00 p.m.** The Matamoros and Jiménez men near the powder house stacked their arms and turned in for sleep. The Aldama and Toluca battalions followed suit.

■ **9:00 p.m.** The San Luis men pulled out of line, ate some hardtack and bedded down.

■ **12:00 a.m.** Santa Anna met with General Castrillón over a midnight meal of chicken and showed little concern for the loss of Mexican lives. Castrillón urged Santa Anna to wait and spare the lives of their men. Santa Anna held up a leg of chicken. "What are the lives of soldiers more than so many chickens." He said, "I tell you, the Alamo must fall, and my orders must be obeyed at all hazards."

■ **12:00 a.m.** The Mexican soldiers were wakened from their sleep at midnight. They assembled their equipment and formed into columns of assault.

■ **1:00 a.m.** Soldiers began moving into their positions. Once across the river, the four columns spread out with each column stationed a musket's shot range from a different wall. After getting into position, the men lay on the ground waiting for the signal to attack. The soldiers huddled close for warmth. They had no ponchos or blankets because of Santa Anna's concerns that such items would slow down the advance.

■ **2:00 a.m.** Santa Anna met with Colonel Juan Nepomuceno Almonte at headquarters, who echoed earlier sentiments about the expenditure of human life. Colonel Almonte said something to Santa Anna about a costly fight, but Santa Anna cut him off: "It doesn't matter what the cost is, it must be done."

■ **3:00 a.m.** The cavalry force saddles up and heads east.

■ **5:00 a.m.** All was in readiness. The attack had been ordered for 4:00 a.m. but the troops were not to move until they heard the bugle signal. Silence was repeatedly ordered and smoking was forbidden.

The Battle

Attack Begins

■ Sometime between 5:00 a.m. and 5:30 a.m., José Maria Gonzales sounded the call to action. The bugler's signal, "*Adenlante!* (Forward!)" rang out and was immediately echoed by all the buglers in the army. Just seconds after the sounds split the morning stillness, 1,200 Mexican soldiers rose in one mass.

■ At the sound of the bugle, swords in hand, officers screamed, "*Arriba!* (Attack!)" The four columns raced across the 200 to 300 yards which separated them from the Alamo walls.

■ As the men advanced, Santa Anna's military bands played "*Deguello.*" *Deguello* meant "cut throat" or "behead," and the music was a hymn of hate and merciless death.

■ Although three sentries had been posted by Travis to watch for the enemy, they apparently fell asleep or failed to detect any unusual movement until it was too late. No alarm was raised.

■ The first man to notice the charge was Captain John J. Baugh. He was the officer of the day and had just begun his rounds at 5:00 a.m. when he heard the bugle, followed by the sounds of distant vivas. He turned to face the plaza and yelled, "The Mexicans are coming!"

■ Upon hearing Captain Baugh's alarm, Travis grabbed his weapons and ran across the plaza to the north wall battery. "Come on boys," Travis called out, "the Mexicans are upon us, and we'll give them hell."

■ The Mexican troops kept breaking out in cheers, which had the unfortunate result of giving away their positions. The Toluca Battalion in the second column northwest of the Alamo yelled out a burst of vivas hailing their republic and their president-general. They paid dearly for it. The gunners at Travis' station touched off a blast of grapeshot. According to Colonel de la Peña, "that cannon volley did away with half the company of *chasseurs* from Toluca."

■ The Toluca Battalion's commander, Colonel Francisco Duque, was hit in the thigh by shrapnel from an Alamo cannon.

■ Travis reached the parapet and discovered the Toluca Battalion was already near the foot of the outside wall. Although the gunners had inflicted terrible damage on the attackers, the Mexicans were so close that the artillery tubes could not be depressed sufficiently to reach them.

■ Mexican soldiers were trapped against the north wall with their enemy overhead and their comrades on every side. Ironically, Mexican bullets took the greatest toll of Mexican lives.

■ Travis leaned over the edge of the parapet to open fire on the enemy and was hit almost immediately. A lead ball struck him in the forehead. He fell back against one of the cannon, still clutching his gun in his hand. Some believe Travis may have been the first to die in the battle.

■ Facing the deadly Texian fire, some Mexican recruits wavered and tried to retreat but the officers and noncoms stood firm. Sergeants beat the men back into the ranks with their thick staffs while officers used the flat of their swords. The men could not have retreated far in any case since Santa Anna had posted lancers to prevent the escape of his own troops as well as the Texians.

■ The fourth column under Colonel Morales made an initial attack against the palisade at the south wall without luck. Crockett's "boys" repelled their assault and they backed off and regrouped to revise their attack plan.

Chaos at the North Wall

■ In the attack on the east wall, Colonel Romero's three hundred riflemen ran into a hail of grapeshot from the artillery mounted at the end of the towering chapel. Their left flank was torn apart and the column swung right in an effort to avoid the fire.

■ On the west wall, General Cós' mass of attacking men were being raked by enemy grapeshot as well as friendly fire from Colonel Duque's column, which was firing haphazardly at the north wall. Cós' men rushed to their left to join with the second column.

■ Repulsed in the first attack, the columns on the east, north and west converged to form a mass of men huddled at the base of the north wall. General Duque was wounded and out of action and command of the north column passed to General Manuel Fernandez Castrillón.

■ Santa Anna saw the three columns massed behind the north wall and believed they were being routed. He panicked and sent in his reserve unit under Colonel Amat to rush the walls along with his whole general staff and everyone else at his side.

■ As a result, four hundred reserves ran toward the Alamo blindly firing their guns. Their high bullets hit the walls, their low bullets raked the heads and shoulders of troops in front of them, bringing down more Mexican soldiers.

Mexicans Enter the Alamo

■ Frustrated by the jumble of men at the north wall, General Cós halted his troops and charged the west wall of the Alamo. He hit the north end and flanked the Texian battery at the northwest angle. Soon the northern rear gate was open and Cós' men poured into the plaza.

■ On the north wall, Mexican soldiers found they could scale the rough wood and stone patch which had been hastily put up to seal the breach in the wall. As they began to climb the wall, the defenders exposed themselves heroically to pour down a deadly fire but Mexican muskets kept up a counter fusillade, sweeping the wall of Texians.

■ Morales' column attacked the southwest corner of the mission and captured the 18-pounder cannon at the point of the bayonet, which they turned upon the interior of the defenses.

Breakout

■ According to William C. Davis in his recent book, *Three Roads to the Alamo*, there are several commonly known sources that indicate a number of men went over the walls and died outside the Alamo—although their importance has long been overlooked. A detailed report of the battle by General Sesma has just been discovered and confirms earlier accounts of Texians leaving the fort and being killed by lancers.

■ Overcome by Mexicans, some of the defenders began to abandon the fortress. General Sesma claimed that a good number came out through the gun emplacement at the northeast corner of the cattle pen. These men leaped over the wall and raced for the brush lining a small ditch. Another fifty Texians went over the wall of the horse corral near the church. They, too, raced for the ditch and chaparral. A third group went over the palisade and through the abatis. Two eyewitness Mexican accounts place the number of men who left the Alamo at sixty-two to sixty-eight, but Sesma's report suggests the number may have been higher. Historian William C. Davis claims that as many as eighty men may have made their way out of the Alamo.

■ General Sesma saw the first breakout of men from the fortress and sent a company of lancers to ride them down in the brush. Sesma testified to "the desperate resistance they posed," but saw his men make short work of them. The second group of about fifty put up an every greater defense, as Ramirez himself saw that the Texians were "ready to sell their lives at a very high price," and he had to send reinforcements twice before his lancers finished them off one by one. The lancers killed all of the men in the last group except one who took refuge in dense brush and had to be shot.

The Fall of the Alamo

■ The intial phase of the battle lasted only about twenty minutes, but it took another hour or so for the Mexicans to clear out the defenders.

■ Once Mexican soldiers overran the plaza, the defenders sought shelter in the barracks. They had spent the past thirteen days preparing these rooms for defense. Parapets blocked the doorways. These were semicircular, made of earth rammed between stretched hides, and just high enough to rest a rifle. Some of the rooms had holes bored into the walls and some even had trenches dug in the dirt floors.

■ Texians fired from the loopholes and doorways at the victorious Mexicans. Those without cover fell in heaps outside. General Juan Amador ordered the cannon by Travis' body to be swung around and used to root out the defenders. The piece was used to blast the barricaded doorways.

■ Santa Anna's men finally stormed the buildings. They moved from doorway to doorway using the same tactics: a shot from the captured cannon to smash the doors and barricades, followed by a storm of musket fire to clear away the defenders, and a final charge to kill any survivors.

■ One by one the buildings were taken, the long barracks to the east, the low barracks on the south, and the collection of huts on the west wall. Most of the killing took place in the long barracks.

■ General Cós became convinced that the Mexican soldiers needed to stop their gunfire in order to reduce their losses. He ordered a Zapadores bugler to blow the cease-fire. It was of no use. The savage shooting continued even after the last defender lay dead.

■ Mexican soldiers found Bowie in his room on the south side of the compound, either dead or dying. Most accounts indicate that Bowie died in bed, that he died alone, and that he did not put up a fight. He was shot in the head and his blood and brains stained the wall behind him.

The Church is Taken

■ After the barracks were overrun, only the church remained. Captain Almeron Dickenson's crew still fired the twelve-pounders on the high platform in back. Bonham joined them, and now only eleven men were left fighting. Below Dickenson's crew in the church, Gregorio Esparza and Robert Evans kept the ammunition coming from the powder magazine by the entrance.

The Fall of the Alamo by Theodore Gentilz. This painting is one of the most accurate portrayals of the Alamo battle. The original was destroyed by fire.
Texas State Library & Archives Commission.

■ Colonel Morales pulled around the captured 18-pounder and began blasting away at the church, the platform, the thick stone walls, and the strong oak doors. Bonham and Dickenson fell in the exchange. The rest of the men on the platform also fell in this manner. Several Mexican accounts say a man took a small child in his arms, ran to the edge of the wall, and jumped to the ground below.

■ The heavy doors of the church splintered under the heavy artillery barrage. The Jiménez and Matamoros men raced through and spread out in the smoke-filled church. Gregorio Esparza quickly fell under their bayonets.

■ Three unarmed gunners from one of the artillery crews sought refuge in the baptistery. Two were shot. The third, Jacob Walker, was tortured. The Mexican soldiers stuck him with bayonets and raised and lowered him several times.

■ Robert Evans tried to kill not only himself but as many others as possible. Travis had ordered that the last man alive or the last to evacuate the fort was to fire the magazine if possible. Believing all was lost, Evans grabbed a torch and headed for the garrison's magazine, where hundreds of pounds of Mexican gunpowder was stored. Evans was stopped by a Mexican bullet only a few feet from the magazine, and died on the floor next to his torch.

■ There are numerous accounts that claim five to seven defenders were either captured or surrendered and were brought to Santa Anna with a request for clemency. Santa Anna ordered the immediate execution of the survivors. Accounts differ as to whether they were shot, bayoneted, or sabered. Several Mexican accounts, including Colonel de la Peña's, state that David Crockett was one of these men. While some historians accept this as true, there are perhaps just as many who question the account.

■ Mexican officers seemed concerned about the women and children. According to Jeffrey Long in *Duel of Eagles*, one of these men stepped to the baptistery and called out, "Is Mrs. Dickenson here? Speak out, for it is a matter of life and death." But when she finally stepped out of the darkness, she was shot in her right calf by one of several wild soldiers. The officer shouted his men back and saved Susannah.

■ The woman and children were removed from the chapel and taken prisoner.

The End of the Battle

■ Showing no remorse for the loss of his own men, Santa Anna pointed at the masses of dead and wounded men and said to Captain Fernando Urizza, "Much blood has been shed; but the battle is over; it was but a small affair."

Chapter Twelve

Bowie, Travis and Crockett

How Did They Die?

James Bowie, William Barret Travis and David Crockett all died at the Alamo. Exactly when, where, and how these brave men lost their lives is not easily determined, for few eyewitnesses lived to tell the story. It is little wonder that a wealth of myth and legend surrounds the deaths of the "Immortal Three."

James Bowie

■ James Bowie had been ill for days, probably of typhoid, but he became dramatically worse on February 24, 1836, and spent the rest of the siege in a small room immediately to the left of the main gate. Mexican soldiers found Bowie in his room on the south side of the compound, either dead or dying. Most accounts indicate that he died in bed, that he was alone, and that he did not put up a fight. He was, however, shot in the head and his blood and brains stained the wall behind him.

■ Not realizing that Bowie was ill and incapacitated, Mexican soldiers believed he was hiding from them while his comrades fought and died outside. A Mexican writer published an account in the Mexico City *El Mosquito Mexicano* on April 5, 1836. In the article, the author wrote, "the perverse and boastful James Bowie died like a woman, almost hidden by covers." The diary of José Juan

James Bowie, Co-Commander of the Alamo. Did Bowie die with a brace of pistols in his hands and his "Arkansas toothpick" in his lap, or was he dead before the battle ever began? *Texas State Library & Archives Commission*

Sánchez-Navarro notes, "Buy [Bowie] the bully, son-in-law of Veramendi died as a coward." It is with no little irony that one of the bravest men in Texas died at the hands of soldiers who believed him to be a coward.

■ Accounts taken from initial interviews with Travis' slave Joe and Susanna Dickenson state that Bowie was killed in his bed and his body mutilated.

■ There were many completely fictitious accounts. Early accounts by two Tejanos, who definitely did not see Bowie die, claim that he took his own life.

■ Juana Alsbury reportedly told Sam Maverick that Bowie was in the upstairs hospital and was carried out into the parade ground and bayoneted. One fanciful story even had Bowie being the only survivor until he got into an argument with a Mexican soldier who had his tongue cut out before throwing him on the burning funeral pyre.

■   The outlandish accounts of Andrea "Madam" Candelaria have all been disproved, and it is widely held that she was not even inside the Alamo. Yet at varying times, she has Bowie fighting from a window with her help, bayoneted in her arms, dying the night before the attack began, and more. In each account she is wounded trying to help him.

William Barret Travis

■   Alerted by the officer of the day, Travis saw the flashes of gunfire on the north wall and ran the seventy yards to the earthen ramp that led up to the gun emplacement. Travis yelled back into the compound, "Come on Boys, the Mexicans are upon us, and we'll give them Hell!" He leaned over the edge of the parapet to take hasty aim and gave the Mexicans both barrels of his shotgun. A volley come back at him and a lead ball struck him full in the forehead. The shot sent him reeling back against one of the cannon. Travis was probably dead by the time he hit the ground.

■   There are two reliable sources to be considered concerning Travis's death. One is Joe, Travis' servant, whose account was recorded by at least two people several days later and all versions substantially agree. The other account, which confirms Joe's story, was penned by an anonymous Mexican soldier in a letter written the day after the battle (March 7, 1836). This account appeared in the Mexico City *El Mosquito Mexicano* on April 5, 1836. "Their leader, named Travis," wrote the Mexican soldier, "died like a brave man with his rifle in his hand at the back of a cannon." The Mexican version of events surrounding Travis' death is the earliest available and probably the most accurate. It also speaks of seeing Travis in death still clutching his gun.

William Barret Travis, Commander of the Alamo. Travis was struck down by an enemy bullet and may have been the first to die. *Texas State Library & Archives Commission*

■ Mayor Francisco Ruiz, who was ordered by Santa Anna to identify the bodies of Travis, Bowie, and Crockett, established the placement of Travis' wound. According to Ruiz, he found Travis' body on a gun carriage, "shot only in the forehead."

More fictitious accounts

■ An initial report by two men, who brought the first news of the battle to Sam Houston, claimed that Travis had died by his own hand. Neither man was an eyewitness, and the location of the fateful wound seems to disprove this theory.

■ Susannah Dickenson often repeated the story that before Travis died, he killed a Mexican general named Mora with his sword. Since this version disagrees with Joe's account, and since Mrs. Dickenson was not in a position to witness Travis' death, her story is not widely accepted. She also seemed confused as to the location of Travis' body, since one account has him at the north wall while another placed him on the top of the church with her husband.

■ Stories circulated that General Cós mutilated Travis' body with his sword (and may have even beheaded him), but these are believed by most historians to be nothing more than rumors. Another story has Santa Anna himself mutilating Travis' body.

David Crockett

■ The greatest controversy surrounds the death of David Crockett. No one who knew Crockett saw him fall and lived to tell of it. "That Crockett fell at the Alamo is all that is known," a visitor concluded sadly a few months later. "By whom or how, no one can tell."

■ Several Mexican accounts, the most notable being Lieutenant Colonel José de la Peña's, claimed that Crockett and four to six others were taken alive, either surrendered or captured, in one of the fortified rooms, and brought before Santa Anna with a request for clemency. Instead he ordered them executed immediately. Depending on whose account you believe, they were either shot, bayoneted, or sabered.

■ There are so many credible accounts about a handful of survivors being executed that many historians accept that such an event took place. However, accounts which claim that Crockett was one of those killed in this manner were written at least several weeks and in some cases more than a year after the fact. Later accounts appear to be derived from earlier ones.

■ The first "account" of Crockett's death was written or dictated by Santa Anna himself less than two hours after the battle. In sending his dispatch to Mexico City, Santa Anna claimed that among the bodies were "Bowie and Travis, who styled themselves Colonels, and also that of Crocket," but mentions nothing of the execution. Many historians believe that he would have mentioned the surrender and execution of Crockett in his report if it had in fact occurred. It is not likely that he would have missed an opportunity to degrade a Texian hero and further humiliate the Texas army.

■ Santa Anna's aide-de-camp, Colonel Juan Nepomuceno Almonte, did not participate in the attack but followed Santa Anna into the Alamo after its fall. Almonte kept a detailed diary whose authenticity remains unchallenged. The diary does not mention anything about survivors who were executed, or anything of Crockett.

■ Many of the Mexican soldiers resented Santa Anna for deserting them at San Jacinto. Others joined the opposition when they saw that Santa Anna was losing political favor in the aftermath of his defeat. Every account of the Crockett surrender-execution story comes from an avowed antagonist (either on political or military grounds) of Santa Anna's. It is believed that many stories, such as the surrender and execution of Crockett, were created and spread in order to discredit Santa Anna and add to his role as villain.

Location of Crockett's body

■ Susannah Dickenson told stories of Crockett being found surrounded by the bodies of dead Mexican soldiers and claimed that he had color in his cheeks even in death. If he died where he was (supposedly) fighting near the palisade, it is possible that she saw his corpse as she was walked to the gate.

■ The first comment on Crockett's death, which is actually attributed to Travis' servant Joe, appears in John Sutherland's 1860 manuscript. Joe reported that Crockett and his Tennesseeans died in the area in front of the church. Joe later stated that "Colonel Crockett had the biggest pile" of dead Mexicans around him.

■ Mayor Francisco Ruiz only added to the confusion. He claimed that he located Crockett's body "toward the west and in the

David Crockett, former
U.S. Congressman from
the state of Tennessee.
Did he survive the fight-
ing only to surrender
and be executed?
*Texas State Library &
Archives Commission*

small fort opposite the city." If he used the north battery as a refer-
ence, that would place Crockett's body in the northwest corner or
farther south near the west wall. Either Mrs. Dickenson and Joe
were mistaken, Ruiz identified the wrong man, he had a false recollection in 1860, or Crockett's body was moved across the compound between the time Susannah saw it and Ruiz arrived.

■ The execution of the men who surrendered most likely took
place in the main plaza, as this is where Santa Anna made a speech
to his victorious soldiers. None of the more reliable sources claimed
to have seen Crockett's body in this area.

■ David Crockett died at the Alamo. That is all we know for
sure.

Chapter Thirteen

Alamo Survivors

It is believed that at least fourteen people survived the fall of the Alamo. There were three Americans: Susannah Dickenson, her daughter Angelina, and Joe (Travis' slave). At least ten Mexican woman and children survived: Juana Alsbury and her baby, her sister, Gertrudis Navarro, Mrs. Gregoria Esparza and her four children, Trinidad Saucedo, and Petra Gonzales. There were probably others who have not been documented.

Santa Anna had his prisoners brought before him one by one.

■ Juana Alsbury, Bowie's sister-in-law, her infant son, and her sister Gertrudis were brought in first. Santa Anna questioned the women about their role in the rebel activities, gave each of them a blanket and two silver pesos, and set them free.

■ Santa Anna closely questioned Senora Esparza. Santa Anna asked, "Where is your husband?" She answered, "He's dead at the Alamo." Santa Anna asked for the names of other people in her family and asked if she was aware that Franciso Esparza, her husband's brother, was a loyal soldier in the Mexican army. She was. Like the other women, the Esparza widow received a blanket and two coins and was dismissed. She returned to her family home in San Antonio.

■ The general also interviewed Susannah Dickenson at length. He was taken with Susannah's daughter, Angelina, and wanted to raise her as his own. With the aid of an interpreter, Santa Anna told Susannah he would raise her daughter as a princess, the child of Mexico's premier leader. Susannah refused and Colonel Almonte interceded on her behalf. Santa Anna questioned her about the rebel army and finally gave her a blanket, two pesos, and let her go.

■ Travis' slave, Joe, received special attention. Santa Anna interrogated him closely. He treated Joe to a grand review of the army and told him it numbered 800,000, hoping this would inspire fear in the rest of the Texian army. By freeing and sparing Joe, Santa Anna sent a message to all slaves in Texas that Mexico was their friend. If they would escape from their masters, they would enter freedom. Some slaves even entered the Mexican army.

■ Mexican deserter Brigido Guerrero was found hiding in the chapel. As the Mexican soldiers came racing up to kill him, he begged for mercy and told them he had been captured and brought into the Alamo against his will. He had tried to escape but to no avail. Incredibly, Guerrero was believed and his life was spared.

Escapes and Departures

■ Regarded as "the only coward in the Alamo," Louis Moses Rose managed to escape before the battle began. As tradition has it, Rose was the only one who failed to cross "Travis' line in the dirt." He allegedly spoke briefly to Bowie and Crockett and went over the wall with a few belongings. Rose was illiterate and told the story to William Zuber's parents, who never wrote it down. William Zuber finally put it in writing many years later. Rose's presence at the Alamo was questioned until evidence was uncovered in 1839 that indicated he was at the Alamo during the siege, and that his testimony was accepted by a local board of Land Commissioners in deciding claims filed on behalf of six different Alamo victims.

■ Evidence suggests that at least one of the defenders escaped. Henry Warnell slipped out of the Alamo and straggled across the prairie. He was badly wounded before or during the escape but made his way to safety. Warnell died of his wounds three months later according to an affidavit filed by his family

■ Twelve men left the Alamo as couriers and did not return before its fall:

James S. Allen
John Walker Baylor
Antonio Cruz y Arocha
Alejandro de la Garza
Benjamin Franklin Highsmith
William P. Johnson
Byrd Lockhart
William Oury
Juan Nepomuceno Seguín
Launcelot Smither
Andrew Jackson Sowell
John Sutherland

■ Recent research indicates that another defender, Samuel Bastian, may also have left the Alamo as a courier.

Chapter Fourteen

Burials, Memorials and Monuments

According to a Texian who visited the Alamo in May 1836, only traces of the three piles of ashes of the Alamo dead could by seen. "The bones had been reduced to cinders, occasionally a bone of the leg or arm was seen almost entire," he wrote. "Peace to your ashes."

Burials

Alamo Heroes Laid to Rest

■ Captain Juan Seguín brought his cavalry to San Antonio in February 1837 to examine what survived of the piles of charred remains. He gave orders that the bells in San Fernando Church should begin to ring, and keep ringing throughout the day.

■ Seguín engaged the services of a San Antonio carpenter to build a coffin. They covered it with black cloth and then placed the ashes from the two smaller piles in the box. Though the contents contained parts of many men, Seguín had the names of Travis, Crockett and Bowie inscribed on the inside of the lid. He laid a Texian rifle and sword atop the casket and had his men carry it to San Fernando Church, and there it remained while a procession gathered in the street outside, the bell ringing all the while.

■ In the late afternoon, Seguín led mourners back through the main street of town, across the San Antonio, and back toward the Alamo and the remaining pile of ashes. The men set the coffin down and Seguín's troopers filed three volleys over it and then did the same thing over the larger pile. His men laid the casket atop of that heap and Seguín addressed the crowd.

> My companions in arms! These remains, which we have had the honor to carry on our shoulders, are the remains of those valiant heroes who died at the Alamo. Yes my friends, they preferred to die a thousand times than to live under the yoke of a tyrant. What a brilliant example! One worthy of inclusion in the pages of history. From her throne above, the spirit of liberty appears to look upon us, and with tearful countenance points, saying, 'Behold your brothers, Travis, Bowie, Crockett as well as all the others. Their valor has earned them a place with all my heroes.' Yes, fellow soldiers and fellow citizens, we are witness to the meritorious acts of those who, when faced with a reversal in fortune, during the late contest, chose to offer their lives to the ferocity of the enemy. A barbarous enemy who on foot herded them like animals to this spot, and then proceeded to reduce them to ashes. I invite all of you to join me in holding the venerable remains of our worthy companions before the eyes of the world to show it that Texas shall be free, and independent. Or to a man we will die gloriously in combat, toward that effort.
> (A recent translation)

■ Following the address, the coffin and remaining ashes were buried on the spot. They fired three more volleys and marched back to town without marking the site. A grove of peach trees grew over the burial place. Within a few years, however, the spot was lost.

Mexican Burials at the Alamo

■ One Alamo defender was not burned on the funeral pyres. A Mexican soldier, Francisco Esparza, presented a personal request to Santa Anna. His brother, Gregoria Esparza, had fought with the rebels and Francisco wanted to spare him from the pyre. Santa Anna allowed him to find his brother's body and give him a proper burial.

■ Many of the Mexican dead did not receive proper burials. Mayor Francisco Ruiz was responsible for carrying the Mexican dead to the cemetery. According to Ruiz, "The dead Mexicans of Santa Anna were taken to the graveyard but, not having sufficient room for them, I ordered some of them to be thrown in the river, which was done the same day."

Monuments

Gonzales Monuments

■ A small monument near Gonzales marks the site of the battle. It was erected in 1903 by the children of Gonzales City Schools. The monument reads:

HERE WAS FIRED THE FIRST GUN FOR TEXAS INDEPENDENCE, OCTOBER 2, 1835.

■ The "Immortal Thirty-two" were honored with their own monument at Gonzales, which reads:

ERECTED IN GRATEFUL RECOGNITION OF THE SUPREME ACT OF HEROISM OF THE THIRTY TWO MEN FROM GONZALES WHO GAVE THEIR LIVES IN THE ALAMO IN RESPONSE TO THE APPEAL FROM TRAVIS.

Alamo Monument

■ The Alamo Cenotaph, a 1936 Centennial memorial to the defenders of the Alamo by the State of Texas, stands in Alamo Plaza. Travis, Crockett, Bowie, and Bonham are depicted, along with other unnamed soldiers. The names of 187 defenders are inscribed on the base.

A Mexican Monument at the Alamo?

■ José Juan Sánchez-Navarro suggested the first Alamo monument. "After the capture of the Alamo, I proposed to the commandant General, Don Marin Perfecto de Cós, that the valiant officers and soldiers who died in the assault be buried in the cemetery of the chapel of the said fort, that the names of each be inscribed on a copper tablet made from one of the cannons captured to be placed on a column at the base of the which these eight lines might be written:

> *The bodies lying here were inspired*
> *By souls, since ascended to heaven,*
> *To savor the glory they'd gained*
> *By the deeds they'd done on earth.*
> *Their last human tribute they paid,*
> *With no fear of death at the end,*
> *For the patriot's death, far from death,*
> *Is transition to greater life.*

My proposal was not accepted."

San Jacinto Monument

■ The San Jacinto Monument was erected by the Federal Government and the State of Texas to commemorate the winning of Texas independence. The shaft is 570 ft. tall and is crowned with a huge Texas star; when illuminated it is visible for many miles.

■ On the eight walls of the building, above which the shaft rises, is carved in bold letters a summary of the colonial history of Texas and the significant results of the battle.

The last paragraph of the inscription reads:

Measured by its results, San Jacinto was one of the decisive battles of the world. The freedom of Texas from Mexico won here led to annexation and to the Mexican war, resulting in the acquisition by the United States of the states of Texas, New Mexico, Arizona, Nevada, Utah, and parts of Colorado, Wyoming, Kansas and Oklahoma. Almost one-third of the present area of the American nation, nearly a million square miles, changed sovereignty.

Chapter Fifteen

Atrocities of War

War atrocities did not begin or end with the Texas War for Independence. The cold-blooded execution of the Goliad prisoners, however, coupled with the slaughter at the Alamo, and merciless massacre of Mexicans at San Jacinto, are unparalleled in the annals of Texas history.

Final Scenes from the Alamo

■ Three unarmed and unidentified gunners from one of the artillery crews sought refuge in the baptistery. Two were shot and killed there. The third, Jacob Walker, was tortured. The Mexican soldiers stuck him with bayonets and raised and lowered him several times, while he cried out for death.

■ Eight-year old Enrique Esparza witnessed the death of perhaps the Alamo's youngest victim. "By my side was an American boy," he said. "He was about my age but larger. As they reached us he rose to his feet. He had been sleeping, but like myself, he had been rudely awakened. As they rushed upon him he stood calmly and across his shoulders drew the blanket on which he had slept. He was unarmed. They slew him where he stood and his corpse fell over me."

■ Even the sick and dying were not spared. The soldiers moved through the hospital killing everyone they found.

■ Felix Nunez fought with Santa Anna. His comrades, Nunez claimed, "became uncontrollable and, owing to the darkness of the building and the smoke of the battle, fell to killing one another, not being able to distinguish friend from foe." Mexican generals advised Santa Anna of this and he mounted a wall believing his presence would put an end to the carnage. It had no effect, and the killing continued.

■ Enrique Esparza confirmed Nunez's story and added a chilling postscript. After the Mexican soldiers had gathered the women and children survivors into a corner of the chapel, they continued to fire at the dead bodies. For fully a quarter of an hour," Enrique later wrote, "they kept firing after all the defenders had been slain and their corpses were lying still."

Alamo Aftermath

■ There are numerous accounts that claim five to seven defenders were either captured or surrendered and brought to Santa Anna with a request for clemency. Santa Anna ordered the immediate execution of the survivors. The accounts differ as to whether they were shot, bayoneted, or sabered. Several Mexican accounts, including one by Colonel José de la Peña, state that Crockett was one of these men. While many historians accept this as true, there are perhaps just as many who question the veracity of the account.

■ Santa Anna inspected the compound and asked to be shown the bodies of Crockett, Bowie, and Travis. He then ordered the faces of the dead wiped clean of grime and smoke, so there would be no confusion between the Mexican and Texian bodies. Once that was done, the soldiers were ordered to collect most or all of the Texians into three piles. The two smaller piles were probably composed of men killed outside the Alamo by lancers, and the larger pile was for the men who fell inside the mission walls. Bodies and wood were stacked in alternate layers. Combustible camphene was poured on the pyres and the fires were lit at 5:00 p.m. The flames were seen at Concepción Mission south of town. The fire burned and smoldered long into the night. The remains lay open to the wind and animals.

■ Cremation was a final, cruel insult to the dead. The practice had all but disappeared from Western Europe by the sixth century because it was believed that the body needed to be whole in order to resurrect upon the Second Coming. The Texians considered Santa Anna's treatment of the Alamo dead as final evidence of his evil.

Goliad Massacre

■ More than 500 prisoners at Goliad fell into Mexican hands following Colonel James Fannin's surrender to General José Urrea. Urrea was ordered to execute the prisoners, but he objected and wrote to Santa Anna recommending clemency. Santa Anna wrote out a final command in triplicate and sent it directly to Colonel José Nicolás Portilla, who was in charge of the prisoners in Goliad. Santa Anna's directive confirmed his desire to execute the rebels. Santa Anna sent Colonel José Vicente Miñon by coach to Goliad to witness the execution.

■ On Palm Sunday, March 27, most of the prisoners were separated into four groups and informed they were to be taken to Matamoros. Singing as they marched, they set out in different directions until ordered to halt. About 15 minutes out of town, the Mexican infantry gunned them down. Mexican lancers cut off many who avoided the repeated volleys while infantrymen finished off the wounded with bayonets and butcher knives.

■ Colonel Fannin heard the firing in the distance and emerged from his room, demanding to know what was happening. When informed that his men were dead and that he was to be shot, he requested that his watch be sent to his family and asked that he receive a proper burial. He gave the commanding officer ten pesos and according to several accounts, asked that they not shoot him in the head.

■ Fannin tied a blindfold over his eyes and sat down in a chair facing the firing squad. He was shot in the head at close range. His body was burned on the pyre with the other victims and the officer in charge pocketed his watch.

■ Careful research has placed the number of killed in the Goliad massacre at 342. The bodies of the Goliad dead were stripped and burned. The corpses in the presidio were carted outside the wall, where four separate pyres were prepared to receive them. Just as at the Alamo, the remains lay exposed to the elements and carnivores for many months afterward.

Revenge at San Jacinto

The slaughter that followed the Battle of San Jacinto on April 21, 1836, was one of the worse war atrocities in U.S. history. The Texians were determined to avenge the loss of those killed at the Alamo and Goliad, and as a result committed offenses almost as vile as the Mexican atrocities. The battle itself lasted no more than eighteen minutes, but the slaughter continued long thereafter. Sam Houston, much like Santa Anna at the Alamo, was unable to control his troops. The number of Mexicans killed in the San Jacinto massacre equaled the number of fallen Texians in the entire revolution. The final count for the day was nine Texians mortally wounded, and some 650 Mexicans killed. About 700 Mexicans escaped the battlefield; 300 were captured before nightfall, and most of the rest were captured over the next two days, including Santa Anna.

■ General Manuel Castrillión directed a Mexican gun crew during the battle. Most of the artillerymen had been killed and the others ran away, calling for the general to come with them. He refused. "I have been in 40 battles and never showed my back," Castrillión yelled. "I am too old to do it now." He turned to face the enemy. Secretary of War Rusk tried to save Castrillión's life by shouting, "Don't shoot him! Don't shoot him!" He even tried knocking some of the rifles aside that were aiming at Castrillión, but others rushed past, took aim, and "riddled him with balls."

■ Sergeant Moses Bryan came across a Mexican drummer boy with both legs broken. The child had grabbed the legs of a soldier and was pleading for his life. Bryan begged the man to spare the child, but he was forced to watch in horror as the unnamed soldier placed a hand on his belt pistol, drew his weapon, and shot the boy.

■ Houston tried to bring order to the killing. He ordered the drum to beat a retreat. No one listened. At last he shouted, "Gentlemen! gentlemen! gentlemen!" he yelled above the din, "I applaud your bravery, but damn your manners!" Then he rode off.

■ Many Mexicans dropped their weapons and ran away. Others fell to their knees and tried to surrender, desperately pleading, "Me no Alamo." Despite their pleas for mercy, they were clubbed and stabbed. Deaf Smith urged the Texians to "take prisoners like the Meskins do!"

■ Upon hearing Houston's orders to take prisoners, one captain called to his men: "Boys, you know how to take prisoners, take them with the butt of yor guns, club guns & remember the Alamo, remember Labaher, & club gun right and left, and nock there brains out."

■ Some of the most cold-blooded slaughter following San Jacinto occurred at Peggy Lake. There, a large number of Mexicans rushed into the twenty-foot-deep water. When the rebels realized what was happening, they took position along the bank and started firing. Although many of the defenseless men were yelling, "Me no Alamo—Me no Goliad," the Texians fired each time any of the enemy "raised their heads out of the water to get a breath." Colonel John Wharton ordered the men to stop firing. J. H. T. Dixon answered, "Colonel Wharton, if Jesus Christ were to come down from heaven and order me to quit shooting Yellowbellies, I wouldn't do it, sir." Dixon cocked his rifle, daring Wharton to enforce his orders. Wharton turned his horse and left.

■   The Mexican dead were not burned or buried, but instead were left where they fell.

Chapter Sixteen

What's in a Name

■ Texans, Texians or Texicans? The early settlers in Texas were usually referred to as colonists or Texians. "Texicans" was used for a time and continued at least up to the time of the Civil War, while "Texan" came into use after the Texas Declaration of Independence was signed.

■ "Tejanos" was a term used to describe a resident of Texas of Hispanic background. Many of these locals would be of great assistance to the Texian army.

■ How did the Alamo get its name? Many believed it took its name from the Spanish Flying Company of the San Carlos De Alamo de Parras, which was sent to reinforce the garrison in 1803. However, "Alamo" literally means cottonwood tree in Spanish, and some historians claim the name came from the nearby cottonwood trees of the Alameda.

■ The Mission San Antonio de Valero, later known as the Alamo, was named for a Mexican saint, Antonio of Padua, and in honor of the Viceroy of Mexico, the Marques de Valero Baltazar de Zuniga.

■ San Antonio de Béxar was the original name of San Antonio. It was most commonly known as "Béxar" during the revolution. The Battle of San Antonio in December 1835 was usually referred to as the "Battle of Béxar."

■ The "War Party" was made up from colonists who sought independence rather than Mexican statehood. They saw themselves as founding fathers of a new republic. Other colonists saw them as troublemakers and called them "War Dogs." The "Peace Party" supported the Mexican Constitution of 1824 and was led by Stephen Austin until he became convinced that war was their only recourse.

■ The Texian army first organized under Stephen Austin was called "The Army of the People." After the Declaration of Independence was signed, it became "the Army of the Republic of Texas."

■ Texians at Goliad held a lottery to pick a good name for their fort. "Milam" and "Independence" were ·popular, but "Defiance" was the winner.

■ Only later would historians refer to the engagement at Gonzales as the Battle of Gonzales. The men who fought there commonly referred to it as the "fight at Williams place."

■ The first cannon shot of the revolution was fired at Gonzales, leading many to refer to that engagement as the "Lexington of Texas."

■ Travis described the Alamo as the "Key to Texas." He arrived in San Antonio on February 3, 1836, and was soon totally committed to its defense. He wrote to Governor Smith, ". . . it is more important to occupy this Post than I imagined when I last saw you—It is the key to Texas."

■ The "Grass Fight" was the name given to an engagement on November 26, 1835. Deaf Smith sighted an enemy column outside of San Antonio and a rumor immediately circulated through camp that the mule train carried a fortune in silver intended to pay the Alamo garrison. Colonel Burleson ordered James Bowie to take a hundred mounted men to reconnoiter the column, but he was not to attack unless he deemed it wise. Most of the volunteers left behind, however, saddled up and followed Bowie, who intercepted the "treasure train" a mile south of San Antonio. Wise or not, Bowie charged the wagons. A short battle ensued before the Mexicans abandoned the pack train and withdrew. Instead of silver, the Texians found only cut grass. The train was only a party that had been sent out that morning to cut fodder for the garrison's starving cavalry horses.

■ The "Runaway Scrape" was the name given to a mass exodus of Texian families who fled their homes and farms in panic as the Mexican army moved eastward. The fall of the Alamo and the massacre at Goliad drove hundreds from their lands. Solders were also afflicted by "runaway fever," and many left the ranks to see to the safety of their families.

■ Stephen Austin was known as the "Father of Texas." He was Texas' first and most successful empresario (land agent). Austin worked throughout his life for the betterment of the colonists and the state. When Austin died on December 27, 1836, the President of the Texas Republic, Sam Houston, issued a proclamation which read: "The Father of Texas is no more! The first pioneer of the wilderness has departed!"

■ Santa Anna considered himself the "Napoleon of the West." He surrounded himself with Napoleonic bric-a-brac. General Filisola wrote that Santa Anna would "listen to nothing which was not in accord with [Napoleon's] ideas."

■ The "Tennessee Mounted Volunteers" were formed in Nacogdoches under the leadership of David Crockett. Interestingly, few of the volunteers were actually from Tennessee; they chose their name to honor their distinguished leader.

■ The "Angel of Goliad," Senora Francisca Alavez, was the wife of a Mexican officer. Her appeals to Colonel Francisco Garay saved a number of prisoners from death. Later, as the

Mexican army advanced eastward, she sent back messages and provisions to the Texians at Goliad.

Colorful nicknames were common among the Texians. . .

■ Sam Houston had several: the Raven, Big Drunk, Governor, General, and the Wanderer.

■ Robert Williamson, one of Travis' close friends and a War Party member, attached a wooden leg to his knee for walking because his right leg was permanently bent back. Williamson was known as "Three-Legged Willie."

■ Pen Jarvis was wounded at the battle of Conception. He was saved from serious injury when an enemy bullet struck the broad blade of his Bowie knife. Thereafter, he was known as "Bowie-Knife Jarvis."

■ Erastus "Deaf" Smith was hard of hearing, but that did not prevent him from providing valuable service to the Texian army as guide, courier, and soldier.

■ John William Smith, a local merchant and Alamo courier, was nicknamed "El Colorado" and "Redhead" the latter for obvious reasons. Smith survived the Alamo and served as a future mayor of San Antonio.

■ Although widely known as "Davy" Crockett, it was not a name he favored.

■ **Many cities and counties throughout Texas are named for some of the Alamo heroes**, including:

Cities:	Counties
Austin	Bowie
Bonham	Burleson
Bowie	Collingsworth
Burleson	Crockett
Crockett	Deaf Smith
Houston	Fannin
Seguin	Houston
Zavala	Maverick
	Milam
	Navarro
	Travis
	Zavala

Chapter Seventeen

Did You Know?

Firsts

■ The first battle in the Texas War for Independence was the Battle of Gonzales on October 2, 1835. The engagement was fought over a small six-pounder cannon, which was shorter than a man's arm and weighed less than 70 pounds. In September 1835, Colonel Domingo Ugartechea, military commander at San Antonio de Béxar, attempted to reclaim the Gonzales cannon, which had been given to the colonists in 1831 for defense again the marauding Indians.

■ The first casualty of the fight was a Texian horseman. When opposing forces exchanged fire, his horse reared and threw him. The rider suffered a bloody nose.

■ The first cannon shot of the revolution was fired on October 2 at Gonzales, leading many to call this battle the "Lexington of Texas."

■ The first Texian to die in the Texas Revolution was Big Dick Andrews, the sole Anglo-American casualty of the fight at Concepción on October 28, 1835. While making his way along a sheltered bank, Andrews brashly cut across the open space above the bluff. The Texians yelled for him to take cover. Every Mexican within range opened fire with a "shower of bullets." Andrews dropped to the ground when a lead ball penetrated his right side and exited his left. Noah Smithwick found Big Dick where he fell and attempted to raise him. "Dick," he cried, "are you hurt?" "Yes, Smith, he replied, "I'm killed; lay me down."

■ The first hero of the revolution was Benjamin Rush Milam. Milam returned from a scouting mission on December 4, 1835 and found the Texian army camped on the outskirts of San Antonio de Béxar, ready to withdraw. It was Milam's call to attack the Mexicans that kept the small army in place, and it was his death on the third day of the Battle of Béxar (December 5-9, 1835) that helped rally the troops to an early victory for the Texians.

■ One of the first volunteer units to come into Texas was the New Orleans Greys, which took its name from the grey colored United States surplus uniforms found in the arsenals of New Orleans. The unit was made up of 100 men from 12 states and six countries. They formed two divisions. One company, commanded by Robert C. Morris, came by boat. The other, under Captain Thomas H. Breece, journeyed overland. After Captain Breece's company crossed the Sabine River, it was presented with an azure blue flag with gold fringe. The men marched to San Antonio and joined the other New Orleans Greys' company in the Battle of Béxar.

■ The first to fall during the battle of the Alamo may well have been William Barret Travis. He was shot in the forehead while defending the north wall at an early hour on March 6. He was twenty-six years old.

Odds and Ends

■ January 1836 found the Texians with a divided government. The problem began when Governor Henry Smith learned through a report from the Alamo commander, Colonel Neill, that the General Council of the provisional government had authorized an expedition on Matamoros. The move left the Alamo

Samuel P. Houston, Commander of the Texian Army. Why did Houston dismiss Travis' pleas for help as "damned lies"? *Texas State Library & Archives Commission*

garrison with a skeleton force of one hundred men and a shortage of provisions and clothing. An outraged Smith proclaimed the Council dissolved and the Council responded by impeaching Smith. In fact, neither Smith nor the Council had been granted the right to depose the other and no one was certain who was in charge.

■ Had it not been for a rainstorm, the Alamo would probably have fallen on February 22, 1836, while the garrison was celebrating Washington's birthday. Only the day before, General Sesma's 1,500-man vanguard reached the Medina River, but the heavy downpour prevented a crossing. At that time only ten men were garrisoned at the Alamo.

■ Alcoholism created serious problems for the Texian army. During the Texian siege of the Alamo in November 1835, many of the volunteers sought relief from the boredom at the bottom of a brown jug. Stephen Austin complained that drunks roared through camp, shooting off rifles and wasting precious powder and ball. "In the name of almighty God," he begged the politicians, "send no more ardent spirits to this camp—if any is on the road turn it back, or have the head [of the barrel] knocked out."

■ According to Jeff Long in his controversial book, *Duel of Eagles*, Santa Anna and Sam Houston were both addicted to opium. At that time, opium was added to many respectable drugs. One of the most popular medicines for a variety of ailments was laudanum, a mixture of opium dissolved in liquor. There appears to be no record of when Santa Anna began taking opium, but several American accounts make it clear that the general swallowed opium—especially in times of stress. When Santa Anna surrendered after the Battle of San Jacinto, the first thing he did was ask for opium. Apparently he asked the right man, for it so happened that Houston was an addict as well. One of Houston's physicians wrote, "he [Houston] had long been accustomed [to it]."

■ Desertion was one of the most serious problems in Houston's army, and Houston was determined to put an end to it. Two deserters were brought up before courts-martial. They were condemned to be shot in front of the whole army, and two graves were dug to hold the corpses. The first deserter was brought out. According to Andrew Briscoe who witnessed the events, "The hole Army was marched to the ground, & the grave was dug & a coffin was there, & the Army was formed in a half circle a round the grave. The man was blindfolded, & made to kneel on the ground by the coffin, & there 12 men to shoot him. The officer gave the command, he said present arms, take ame. Just at that moment, Colonel Hockley was coming in a lope from camp, halloing, halt, halt, halt, & the officer said order arms. Colonel Hockley rode up and said Lieutenant here is repreave."

Unknown to the men, the entire execution had been staged; the message, however, was clear.

■ The capture of a Mexican courier may have led to the Texian victory at San Jacinto. On April 18, 1836, scouts Henry Karnes and "Deaf" Smith returned with a captured Mexican courier who carried letters addressed to Santa Anna with valuable information. The courier was obviously a veteran of the Alamo, for the dispatches were in deerskin saddlebags marked "William Barret Travis." Santa Anna, claimed the dispatches, was personally at the head of small force in New Washington and isolated from the rest of the army. Houston realized that if the war were to be won he would have to strike Santa Anna before he could receive reinforcements. The next day Houston's army departed Harrisburg. "We are in preparation to meet Santa Anna," Houston wrote to his friend Henry Raquet. "It is the only chance of saving Texas."

■ Sam Houston received a gift from Santa Anna when he spared the Mexican general's life. The inscription in Santa Anna's gold snuffbox reads as follows:

"We the children of Sam Houston wish
to present to you our kinsman, Henry Houston, as a
slight token of our esteem, the accompanying
gold snuff box which was once the property of
our father and greatly prized by him. It was
presented to him by Santa Anna, the Mexican President
and commander, after his defeat by the Texan army at
San Jacinto, as a token of gratitude, we suppose for our
father's intercession in his behalf, when his life was
threatened by Texan soldiers and civil officers.

I am, my dear sir, with sincere regard,
(signed) Maggie Houston Williams
Independence, Texas   May 25, 1895

Doubt and Disbelief

■ Apparently Sam Houston was one of the few who didn't seem to take Travis' pleas seriously. He had pledged to exert all "mortal power" to "relieve the brave men in the Alamo" but took his time getting to Gonzales, where he was going to raise a relief force. He left the Convention on March 6, and it took Houston five days to complete a journey that should have taken no more than two days. By that time the Alamo had fallen, but Houston had no way of knowing this.

■ On March 7, Houston wrote a letter to James Collinsworth expressing doubt that the Mexicans were even in San Antonio—despite all of Travis' dispatches and the eyewitness testimony of couriers.

■ Houston stopped at Burnham's Crossing on the way to Gonzales. According to a Texian settler, W. W. Thompson, Houston lingered at Burnham's "all night and all that day and all night again." When Thompson asked Houston's opinion concerning the siege of the Alamo, Houston "swore that he believed it to be a damn lie, & that all those reports from Travis and Fannin were lies, for there were no Mexican forces there and that he believed that it was only electioneering schemes on [the part of] Travis & Fannin to sustain their own popularity."

■ Houston arrived in Gonzales on March 11 and was forced to confront the truth. Travis' reports had not been lies or exaggerations after all.

Texas Independence

■ The Convention at Washington decided unanimously for a Declaration of Independence on March 2, 1836. Although Travis and his men died without knowing that the independence for which they had been fighting had been declared, they were represented in that vote: Sam Maverick and Jesse Badgett,

Travis' elected delegates, were there to sign their names to the document.

Battle Scenes

■ Dr. Launcelot Smither had an interesting experience early in the war. Smither rode out to Gonzales on October 1, 1835, in an attempt to prevent bloodshed. Smither was told to report to the Mexican camp and inform them that the Texians would not attack that night. The Mexicans met Smither's arrival with apprehension. He was placed under guard and his mules, money, and belongings were confiscated. The next morning the Mexican commander dispatched Smither to the Texian camp with a request for a meeting. Dr. Smither delivered the message but was immediately arrested and taken to the rear. Dr. Smither was taken prisoner by both sides that morning while serving the cause for peace.

■ Captain Don Nicolás Rodriguez, post commander at Lipantitlan, found himself in an embarrassing situation. Rodriquez and the bulk of the garrison departed Lipantitlan for Goliad on October 31 to harass the rebels at Goliad. Ironically it was the same day the Texians at Goliad sent out their expedition to take Lipantitlan under the command of Adjutant Ira J. Westover. Captain Rodriguez had almost reached Goliad when he learned that Westover had taken possession of his garrison at Lipantitlan. The captain immediately turned around and headed back.

■ Sam Houston was almost removed from command. The interim government at Harrisburg was dissatisfied with Houston's course of continued retreat. In early April 1836, President Davis G. Burnet sent Secretary of War Rusk to deliver a letter to Houston: "Sir: The enemy are laughing you to scorn. You must fight them. You must retreat no further. The country expects you to fight. The salvation of the country depends on your doing so." If Houston refused to attack, Rusk was authorized to assume command of the army. However, Rusk determined that Houston had acted properly and supported Houston. Rusk ended up staying with the army, not just to oversee Houston but to become a part of it.

■ Santa Anna and his troops were caught napping at the Battle of San Jacinto. When Houston failed to attack on the night of April 20 and again on the morning of April 21, Santa Anna believed the Texians were in no hurry to attack. In the late afternoon, Santa Anna gave his weary troops permission to rest and retired to his camp bed. Houston attacked at 4:30 p.m. and caught the Mexicans completely unawares. The Mexicans panicked and fell back. The battle was over in eighteen minutes, but the slaughter continued for hours.

■ Houston's horse, Saracen, was hit by five balls at San Jacinto before dropping to the ground. Houston's second horse also went down, and a musket ball struck Houston in his Achilles' heel and shattered his right ankle. He managed to mount a third horse and draped his wounded leg over the saddle pommel.

■ Santa Anna nearly escaped following his defeat at San Jacinto. He was chased by rebel cavalry and lost his horse about seven miles from the field. He hid in a thicket of pines and changed his clothes. The next day a search party found him and took him back to camp not realizing they had captured Santa Anna. When they approached the Mexican prisoners, every Mexican officer rose to his feet and the troops called out, "El Presidente." The surprised Texians immediately took the captured general to Sam Houston.

Unfurled Banners

■ One of the first Texas battle flags was raised during the battle of Gonzales in October 1835. It was made of white silk from a wedding dress. An image of the disputed Gonzales cannon barrel was painted in black paint. Underneath appeared the challenge: "COME AND TAKE IT." The 32 men who came from Gonzales to aid the Alamo carried the Gonzales flag with them.

■ The New Orleans Greys crossed the Sabine to join the Texas Revolution. Upon their arrival they were presented with an azure blue banner, fringed with gold. Bold black letters proclaimed, "FIRST COMPANY OF TEXAN VOLUNTEERS! FROM NEW ORLEANS!" In the center of the flag a flying eagle bore the proud legend "God & Liberty." This was the only Texian banner taken from the Alamo on March 6 and is still held in Mexico today.

■ The tri-color Lone Star flag (known as the Sarah Dodson flag), was made by the wife of Lt. Archelous Dodson, an officer who was organizing a company of Harrisburg, Texas volunteers. The flag was made of blue, white, and red calico squares of equal size. The blue square, bearing a five-pointed white star in its center, was placed next to the flagstaff. This flag went into service in September 1835.

■ Joanna Troutman, often called the Betsy Ross of Texas, was only eighteen when she helped organize the Georgia Battalion of volunteers that left for Texas late in 1835. As the men prepared to leave, she presented them with her "Lone Star" flag of silk, blue on white, with a five-pointed star subscribed "Liberty or Death." Most of the Georgia Battalion was attached to Colonel Fannin's command and was massacred at Goliad. The flag was ripped to pieces after the battle, but the symbol of the Lone Star would remain.

■ The San Jacinto battle flag was made by the Ladies' Auxiliary in Kentucky. Sidney Sherman's volunteers brought it to Texas. It was the only flag that waved over the Texian army at San Jacinto. It was stored in a wooden chest for many years, but was restored for the Texas Centennial celebration in 1936. The restoration was not entirely authentic. The figure of liberty, originally draped in a way to appeal to the soldiers, is now clad in a somewhat more chaste manner.

■   Travis ordered a flag raised from a makeshift shaft when he saw the head of the Mexican column arrive in San Antonio. It may have been the flag he bought in San Felipe for $5.00, of which no description remains. The Mexicans believed it was the national tricolor, with two stars in the middle for the two states of Coahula and Texas, but the best evidence indicates this is not the case. The Texians were fighting for independence and would not have flown a Mexican banner.

■   The Mexican battle flag was red, white and green with the picture of an eagle, the symbol of the Central Government.

■   The Mexicans raised a "blood red" flag on the Alamo side of the San Fernando Church belfry when they arrived in San Antonio on February 23. It was plainly visible and signified no mercy would be given to the trapped garrison. Santa Anna told his staff repeatedly in San Antonio, "I neither ask for nor give quarter."

■   A second red banner was raised in San Antonio on Powder House hill to the east on March 4. The message to the Texians was clear: no prisoners would be taken.

■   Near the end of the battle of the Alamo, a Mexican soldier named José Maria Torres climbed to the top of the Alamo barracks and pulled down the Texian flag. He raised the Mexican tricolor of the Zapadores (corps of engineers) in its place just before he was shot and mortally wounded.

Music

■ One of Crockett's favorite ways to cheer the men during the siege was to stage a musical duel between himself and John McGregor. The "Colonel" had found an old fiddle and challenged McGregor to get out his bagpipes and see who could make the most noise. McGregor always won.

■ At San Jacinto, Houston and his army advanced to the sounds of "Come to the Bower," a tune regarded as quite risque. A German who could play the fife and a Negro freedman who could beat a drum played along with two other musicians who also volunteered. But this foursome only knew popular music of the day:

"Will you come to the bow'r I have shaded for you?
Our bed shall be roses all spangled with dew.
There under the bow'r on roses you'll lie
With a blush on your cheek but a smile in your eye."

■ Santa Anna's military bands played "Deguello" as their men advanced on the Alamo on the morning of March 6. The word meant "cut throat" or "behead," and the music was a hymn of hate and merciless death.

Myths and Legends

■ *Buying Time*. Travis did not buy time for Houston or anyone else by holding off the Mexican advance for thirteen days, although tradition would have you believe otherwise. According to William C. Davis in *Three Roads to the Alamo*, Santa Anna remained in front of the Alamo because he wanted to. "An army the size of his could have marched around the Alamo and on to the Mexican interior," explained Davis, "with no fear of leaving 200 or so Texians in a mud fort in his rear." One regiment or a few companies of lancers could have contained the garrison and eliminated them from any role in the campaign.

■ *Travis' New Uniform.* Travis had ordered a uniform from McKinney and Williams, but his letter of January 21, 1836 to Captain W. G. Hill, mentions that it wasn't very far along. He left for the Alamo on January 23, so there is little chance that it caught up to him before the siege. Sergeant Felix Nunez, who took Travis' coat after the battle, said that is was made of home-spun Texas jeans.

■ *The Line in the Dirt.* There is little evidence to confirm that Travis actually drew his now-famous line in the dirt. Travis assembled his men for a meeting and according to legend, drew a line in the dust with his saber, inviting all who wished to stay and die with him to cross that line. The alleged witness, Louis Rose, was illiterate and told the story to William Zuber's parents who never wrote it down. William Zuber finally put it in writing. There was no mention of Travis' line by anyone until Zuber's account was published.

■ Apparently Travis did gather his men for a conference. Mrs. Dickenson remembered that Travis "asked the command that if any desired to escape, now was the time to let it be known, and to step out of ranks." Shortly thereafter Louis Rose is said to have escaped, which may mean that Travis may have told each man to decide for himself. There is still disagreement over whether the line was actually drawn, but as Walter Lord asutely wrote in *A Time to Stand*, "what harm in a legend that only serves to perpetuate the memory of valor and sacrifice."

■ *The Washington Birthday Ball.* According to one tradi-tion, Santa Anna attended the Washington's Birthday ball held in San Antonio on February 22 in civilian clothes. It is said that he gathered valuable information while conversing with the guests. The tale is unlikely, since several of the people in attendance, in-cluding the Seguíns, would have recognized the general. The story probably originated from other adventures in earlier campaigns. It is said that Santa Anna once dressed as a woman to reconnoiter enemy positions, and on another occasion escaped from an enemy-held town by openly boasting that he had just won a great victory.

■ *Santa Anna's Mock Wedding.* During the siege of the Alamo, it is said that Santa Anna found himself desiring the company of a local senorita. Her mother was angry at his advances towards her daughter and insisted on marriage. One of his officers arranged for a Mexican soldier to imitate a priest and a marriage was performed. Legend has it that Santa Anna spent part of his time during the siege enjoying his honeymoon. After the battle, he dispatched his new wife to one of his estates, where she delivered his child. According to Albert Nofi in *The Alamo and The Texas War for Independence*, much of this story is certainly false. The young woman and her mother would have known that Santa Anna was already married. However, there was apparently a young lady in San Antonio that the general passed his nights with and who eventually did bear his child. Any objections to the liaison seem to have been overcome by a gift of 2,000 pesos.

■ *Santa Anna and the Yellow Rose of Texas.* Many reasons have been given for Santa Anna's poor performance at San Jacinto, including opium, a heavy lunch, and a hot day. But the most interesting is the story of Emily Morgan, a young mulatto girl, with whom it is said that Santa Anna spent much of the afternoon. There are even versions of the tale that claim Sam Houston sent Morgan to Santa Anna's camp in an attempt to distract him. While the story is not mentioned in early and generally reliable accounts, it has been accepted by a number of Mexican historians. While Santa Anna may have spent some time with the girl, it is unlikely that Houston had a hand in the events. The story of Emily Morgan is the basis of the old song, "The Yellow Rose of Texas." It is not well known that the "yellow" refers to Morgan's coloring.

■ *The Masonic Distress Signal.* It has been said that Sam Houston spared the life of Santa Anna because the general gave the Masonic Distress Signal and that it was recognized and respected. Jeff Long in *Duel of Eagles* claims it is more likely that Houston did not execute Santa Anna because of the effects of opium. Houston's doctor had sedated him with opium for his wounded ankle, and he woke from his opiated nap and appeared mellow and forgiving.

Chapter Eighteen

Numbers and Statistics

Nearly 10,000 men risked their lives in the conflict that would forever alter the course of Texas, American, and Mexican history. Soldiers on both sides fought valiantly and died with honor. More than 1,600 made the ultimate sacrifice.

Numbers and Losses of Various Battles

Gonzales – October 2, 1835

■ Lieutenant Francisco Casteñada and 100 dragoons arrived in Gonzales on September 29. They faced only eighteen Texians, but calls went out for reinforcements and by October 1, the Texians had increased their number to 180.

■ The first casualty of the Texas Revolution was a Texian horseman. When the vanguards of the opposing forces exchanged fire, his horse reared and threw him. The rider suffered a bloody nose.

■ *Texian casualties*: One bloody nose.

■ *Mexican casualties*: Small, with no more than one or two killed.

Goliad – October 9, 1835

■ A militia company of twenty men, under the command of Captain George Collinsworth, was formed at Matagorda on October 6, 1835 to oppose the Mexicans. Captain Collinsworth sent word to surrounding settlements for men to join him on the expedition. Settlers from across the prairie responded to the call. It is believed he may have had as many as 125 men by the time he reached Goliad.

■ The Mexican troops at Goliad under Captain Francisco Sandoval consisted of three officers and about fifty enlisted men, a force too small to defend even the perimeter of the presidio.

■ The presidio of La Bahia at Goliad was won in less than 30 minutes.

■ *Texian casualties*: One shoulder wound.

■ *Mexican casualties*: All were taken prisoner.

Concepción – October 28, 1835

■ On a detached assignment, Colonel Bowie and ninety-two men faced General Cós and his force of 300 dragoons and 100 infantrymen.

■ The first fatal casualty of the revolution was at Concepción. Richard Andrews brashly exposed himself to enemy fire. The Texians yelled for him to take cover, and every Mexican within range opened on him. A lead ball struck Andrews in his right side and exited out his left, mortally wounding him.

■ *Texian casualties*: One killed.

■ *Mexican casualties*: Seventy-six killed or wounded. The survivors fled.

The Alamo

■ Some 1,600 Mexicans assaulted the Alamo on March 6. The actual battle lasted only 20 minutes, but it took another hour for the Mexicans to clear out the remaining defenders.

How Many Defenders Died at the Alamo?

■ The traditional number of 182 came from Mayor Francisco Ruiz, who was in charge of burning the bodies. Presumably, this figure only represented those burned in the pyres in or near the compound, and would not include the body of Gregorio Esparza, the only defender Santa Anna allowed to be buried. It also did not include the sixty-two to sixty-eight men who were killed outside the walls, since it is doubtful they would have been moved to the larger pile. These men were probably burned in the smaller pyres. Therefore, it is reasonable to add at least sixty to the traditional number, which suggests a possible total of 243. This closely matches the rough estimates of 250 stated by several eyewitnesses.

■ Santa Anna reported to his government that the enemy dead totaled more than 600.

Mexican Casualties

■ Mexican casualties were high. According to William C. Davis in *Three Roads to the Alamo,* of the 1,600 men involved in the attack, about 400 were wounded, including one general and twenty-eight officers. Seventy-five of these wounds proved mortal. The exact number killed in battle is not known, but some of the Mexican eyewitnesses estimated the number of dead at 200.

The Texians (and by many accounts, the Mexicans themselves) inflicted 38 percent casualties on the attacking troops in less than an hour.

Goliad

■ Sam Houston ordered Colonel Fannin to withdraw from Goliad. Delays and mismanagement resulted in Fannin's men being captured at Coleto Creek.

■ Best estimates indicate Fannin had some 350–400 men. Mexican forces were estimated at 400.

■ *Texian Casualties*: Estimated at nine dead and fifty-one wounded. All survivors were taken prisoner.

■ *Mexican Casualties*: Estimated at fifty killed and 140 wounded.

San Jacinto

■ On March 12, 1836, Houston organized his army of about 400 men into the 1st Volunteer Regiment. By early April, Houston's army numbered about 1,100 men. He left some 250 men at Harrisburg to guard supplies and moved on to San Jacinto with 800-850 men.

■ The Mexican forces under Santa Anna totaled about 1,250 men according to the Mexican army rolls. However, total Mexican casualties reported by Houston indicate a much larger number.

■ Houston calculated the battle lasted only eighteen minutes from the first shot to the capture of the camp. The slaughter thereafter continued for hours.

■ Colonel Almonte managed to gather 400 soldiers together for a mass Mexican surrender.

■ Seven hundred Mexicans escaped the battlefield, but 300 were captured before nightfall. The rest were captured over the next two days.

■ *Texian Casualties*: Nine dead and twenty-six wounded.

■ *Mexican Casualties*: 650 killed (the number of surviving wounded, if any, is not known). The rest were taken prisoner.

■ Almost as many Mexicans were killed at San Jacinto as Texians in the entire revolution.

Combined Numbers and Losses in the War for Texas Independence

Texian Forces:

■ Some 3,500 to 3,600 men served in the Revolutionary forces, including the Navy, at some time during the war, but not all at the same time. Some, for example, served only a few days.

■ At the time of the siege of the Alamo, the principal contingents of the Texas army totaled about 1,900 men:

■ **Alamo:** 200-250 men organized into five companies of volunteers, one of Travis' cavalrymen (the only one raised), and one of artillerymen.

■ **Goliad:** 465 men organized into one company of regulars consisting of two battalions of five companies each plus an odd half-company and fifteen miscellaneous volunteers. Average company size was about thirty-eight men.

■ **Refugio:** 150 men constituting the Matamoros expedition.

■ **Gonzales:** 275 men in the main army plus 100 more on their way with Houston, comprising about eight miscellaneous companies.

■ Other forces: 650 or more, with troops at Velasco, Matagorda, and scattered across the frontier.

Texian Casualties:

■ The Texians suffered about 25% casualties with about 17% dead.

■ Total casualties were about 850-950. Best estimates are 600 killed, an incredibly high figure given the numbers involved. The heavy causalities, of course, stem from the 350 men slaughtered with Fannin, and the 183-250 massacred at the Alamo.

Mexican Forces:

■ Santa Anna entered Texas with some 6,100 men. After San Jacinto, General Filisola reported his effectives totaled 4,078.

Mexican Casualties:

■ The Mexicans suffered about 34% casualties and about 17% dead.

■ Total casualties were about 2,100. Best estimates are 1,000 dead, 700 prisoners, and 400 wounded.

■ The heavy casualties are largely the result of the 650 men killed at San Jacinto.

Battles

■ *Longest Battle: San Antonio [Béxar] – December 5-9, 1835.*

■ *Shortest Battle: San Jacinto – 18 minutes, April 21, 1836.*

Cost of the Texas War for Independence

■ By the end of August 1836, the war had cost Texas about $1,250,000.

■ Approximately $25,000 was raised through voluntary donations from people in Texas.

■ Additional monies were received from the states but the amounts are not known.

■ Most of the monies came from loans or promissory notes. Many of the loans were eventually paid off in land.

■ At the time of his death, the Republic of Texas owed Travis $143 for his out-of-pocket expenditures.

■ According to Albert Nofi in *The Alamo*, the breakdown of expenses were as follows:

Army	$412,000
Navy	$112,000
Supplies	$450,000
Civil Expenditures	$118,000
Interest	$100,000
Miscellaneous	$ 60,000

The State of Texas:

Population of Texas, 1834

■ According to a survey conducted by Colonel Juan Almonte, the population in Texas north of the Nueces River seemed to have been about 36,000 people:

■ Americans: Whites, 15,400; Blacks, 2,000; Indians, 4,500 (settled), and 10,500 ("wild"); Mexicans, 3,600.

■ Population of San Felipe: 2,900

■ Population of San Antonio: 2,400

■ Population of Nacogdoches: 4,000

Texas Boundaries

■ In 1836, the Republic of Texas claimed some 360,000 square miles. After annexation, it would encompass almost 100,000 square miles less.

■ In 1819, a treaty established an eastern and northern line between Spain and the United States that essentially followed the Sabine, Red, and Arkansas rivers, and then extended west to the Pacific Ocean. Texas' western boundary with Mexican remained vague until the Republic defined it as the Rio Grande from its mouth to its source, then north to the 42nd parallel.

■ After annexation and war with Mexico, the United States in 1850 established the boundary east from above El Paso, along the 32nd parallel to the 103rd meridian, up to latitude 36 degrees 30 (the line between slave and free states set by the Missouri Compromise); east to the 100th meridian and south to the Red River.

Bibliography

Chariton, Wallace O. *Exploring the Alamo Legend*. Texas: Wordware Publishing, Inc., 1992.

—. *One Hundred Days in Texas*. Texas: Wordware Publishing, Inc., 1990.

Clark, J. L. *A History of Texas*. D. C. Heath and Company, 1940.

Daughters of the Republic of Texas. *The Alamo Long Barrack Museum*. Dallas, Texas: Taylor Publishing Co., 1986.

De la Peña, José Enrique. *With Santa Anna in Texas*. College Station: Texas A&M University Press, 1997.

Davis, William C. *Three Roads to the Alamo*. New York: Harper Collins, 1998.

Fehrenbach, T. R. *Lone Star*. New York: American Legacy Press, 1983.

Groneman, Bill. *Alamo Defenders*. Austin, Texas: Eakin Press, 1990.

—. *Eyewitness to the Alamo*. Republic of Texas Press, 1996.

Guerra, Many Ann Noonan. *The Alamo*. The Alamo Press, 1996.

Haley, James L. *Texas*. New York: Doubleday & Company, Inc., 1985.

Hardin, Stephen L. *Texian Iliad*. Austin: University of Texas Press, 1994.

Haythornewaite, Philip. *The Alamo and the War of Texas Independence 1835-1836*. London: Osprey, 1996.

Long, Jeff. *Duel of Eagles*. New York: Quill, William Morrow, 1990.

Lord, Walter. *A Time to Stand*. Lincoln and London: University of Nebraska Press, 1978.

Matovina, Timothy M. *The Alamo Remembered*. Austin: University of Texas Press, 1995.

Nelson, George. *The Alamo*. Dry Frio Canyon, Texas: Aldine Press, 1998.

Nevin, David. *The Texans*. New York: Time-Life Books, 1975.

Nofi, Albert A. *The Alamo*. New York: Da Capo Press, 1994.

Tinkle, Lon. *The Alamo*. New York: The New American Library, 1960.

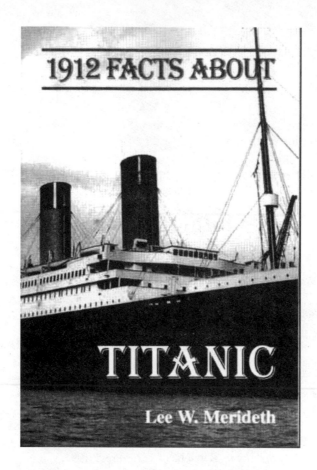

1912 FACTS ABOUT
TITANIC
Lee W. Merideth

If you enjoyed Mary Deborah Petite's

1836 FACTS ABOUT
THE ALAMO
& THE TEXAS WAR FOR INDEPENDENCE. . .

experience TITANIC,
the FIRST book in our "Facts About" series!

An EXCLUSIVE excerpt
from the chapter "Destiny," is reprinted on the following pages. . .

■ Third Class passenger Eugene Daly spent a good portion of Friday, Saturday and Sunday out on the aft well deck playing his bagpipes.

■ Meanwhile, Benjamin Hart and his daughter Eva spent much of Sunday exploring the ship while Eva's mother slept in the cabin. She had been up all night waiting for some catastrophe to happen to them and the *Titanic*.

■ Down in the Third Class common areas there was some sort of dance every night with music provided by the many musically inclined passengers.

■ Pretty much the same routine was followed every day by the passengers. When the weather permitted it, many spent a large portion of the daylight hours out on the open decks and whatever event occupied their time would give way to meal call when Mr. P.W. Fletcher made his appearance with his bugle.

ICE WARNINGS

■ The winter of 1912 was one of the mildest in over thirty years and this warm weather allowed huge chunks of ice to break off Greenland's ice fields and drift south into the North Atlantic shipping lanes. These shipping lanes were routinely moved further south at this time of year because of the potential for icebergs, but in 1912, even ships steaming in these southern lanes reported an increasing amount of ice.

Some of the ice resembled huge buildings or mountains and icebergs 100 feet tall weren't uncommon. There were also miles of sheet ice (also called field ice), ice that was ten or twenty or thirty feet thick and which no ship could penetrate without much low speed maneuvering. Most ships had to steer many miles out of their way to get around the ice and then only in the daylight.

There were also the growlers, smaller icebergs that broke off from the larger ones. All-in-all, the huge ice pack that was floating down from Greenland that April extended over 70 miles north-to-south, and it was sitting right in the middle of the main shipping lanes. The ice pack was so extensive that ships either had to stop for it or steam even further south. Neither option was considered good by Captain Smith.

■ Ice warnings were received by the wireless operators even before *Titanic* left Southampton. Between Thursday and Saturday over twenty ships reported ice in the area *Titanic* would be steaming. Many ships were forced to stop once they entered the ice field, and most of them had to stop at night to prevent a collision with an iceberg. This was pretty much standard practice for ships of the time.

On Friday morning the ship *Empress of Britain*, eastbound from Halifax to Liverpool reported ice. (This and all future ice warnings listed here were picked up by *Titanic's* wireless operators, either directly or passed on from another ship. The wireless operators would then pass the massages onto the ship's officers.)

That afternoon, *La Touraine*, eastbound from New York to Le Havre reported ice.

In all, there were ten warnings on Friday alone about ice in the area of 41° 41' N latitude. Ships all along the shipping lane reported ice, most of it right in the area *Titanic* was scheduled to cross on Sunday night.

■ On Saturday there were over a dozen ice warnings received by wireless operators Phillips and Bride, who were now fully occupied in trying to work through the backlog of messages created when the wireless broke down the night before.

■ Sunday, April 14 was a beautiful day to be steaming across the North Atlantic. The weather was perfectly clear and the seas calm. The outside temperature was such that many passengers spent most of the day on the promenade decks to enjoy the sun. The air temperature wasn't overly warm, raising only to the mid-50's during the day, but for the passengers coming from the winter months in the colder climates, the temperature was perfectly fine.

There was a White Star Line requirement that all liners conduct a lifeboat drill on Sunday morning after Services, but for some reason Captain Smith did not hold one this day.

■ **9:00 a.m.:** The day's first ice warning was received from *Caronia*, eastbound from New York to Liverpool. This message was directed to *Titanic* instead of being the usual general warnings directed to all ships: *"Captain, Titanic—West-bound steamers report bergs, growlers and field ice in 42° N, from 49° to 51° W, April 12, Compliments, Barr."* This warning was passed onto Captain Smith, who posted it for his officers to read and take note of.

■ **10:30 a.m.:** Religious services were held in the First Class Dining Saloon.

■ **11:40 a.m.:** *Noordam* signaled to *Titanic*, "Much ice."

■ **12:00 noon:** The ships officers gathered to "shoot the sun" and take the noon position bearings. They also calculate the previous 24 hour distance of 546 miles. This information was posted in the First Class Lounge for all those taking bets on the previous day's progress.

■ **1:42 p.m.:** *Baltic*, eastbound from New York to Liverpool, relayed a message: "...*Greek steamer Athinai reports passing icebergs and large quantities of field ice today in latitude 41° 51' N, longitude 49° 52' W... wish you and Titanic all success. Commander.*"

This message was handed to Captain Smith, who in turn handed it to Bruce Ismay with whom he was speaking at the time. Ismay put the message in his own pocket instead of passing it onto the bridge officers. A look at the map would have shown that *Titanic* was headed right into the mass of this ice field.

■ **1:45 p.m.:** A private message was relayed from *Amerika* through *Titanic's* wireless to the US Hydrographic Office that *Amerika* had passed several large icebergs in the same area reported by the *Athinai*. This message was not passed onto the bridge.

During the afternoon the temperature had steadily declined to 43 degrees at 5:30 p.m., but between then and 7:30 p.m. it dropped another 10 degrees to 33 degrees. Because of the rapid drop in temperature, most of the passengers moved inside for the remainder of the afternoon.

■ **5:20 p.m.:** There was a planned change of course that was to be made at this time to bring the ship to a more westerly direction from its current generally southwesterly direction. Captain Smith held off making this change for a few minutes in order to bring *Titanic* even further south, apparently in order to avoid the ice that was reported to be in the area of *Titanic's* original course.

■ **5:50 p.m.:** Captain Smith ordered the delayed course change which the officers thought would put *Titanic* south and west of any of the reported ice.

■ **6:00 p.m.:** Lightoller relieved Wilde on the bridge. Sixth Officer Moody shared the watch with him.

■ **7:15 p.m.:** During dinner, Ismay showed the *Baltic* ice warning message to several passengers and by now Captain Smith had retrieved it and posted it in the chart room.

■ **7:15 p.m.**: It was dark outside and very cold, just a couple degrees above freezing. First Officer Murdoch ordered lamp trimmer Samuel Hemming to secure the forward forecastle hatch and the skylight over the crew's galley to prevent light from reflecting up into the eyes of the lookouts in the crow's nest who were now on special alert to spot any ice.

■ **7:30 p.m.**: A message was intercepted from *Californian* to *Antillian*: *"To Captain, Antillian: Six-thirty p.m....latitude 42° 3' N, longitude 49° 9' W, Three large bergs, 5 miles to the southward of us. Regards. Lord."* This message was delivered by Marconi operator Bride to one of the officers on the bridge, but he later couldn't remember which officer.

The message wasn't passed on to Captain Smith either. He was down in the à la carte restaurant having dinner with the Wideners and several other First Class passengers. *Titanic* was steaming directly into this ice field, and it was only 50 miles away.

■ **7:30 p.m.**: Lightoller "shot the stars" and gave the information to Boxhall who updated the plot. If anyone had remembered to mark *Californian's* warning on the chart, it would have been obvious that *Titanic* was entering dangerous waters.

■ **8:00 p.m.**: Lightoller decided to check Moody's navigational skills by having him plot the estimated time *Titanic* would enter the area of the icefield. Moody estimated around 11:00 p.m., but Lightoller wasn't happy with that answer. He had already figured the time to be around 9:30 p.m.

■ **8:40 p.m.**: While Reverend Carter was conducting his evening hymn singing down in the Second Class Dining Saloon, the temperature was continuing to fall. Lightoller ordered the ship's carpenter to check the fresh water supply because there was a very good chance that it might freeze.

■ **8:55 p.m.**: Captain Smith returned to the bridge after his dinner with the Wideners and engaged Lightoller in a conversation, speaking about the weather. Lightoller later reported:

> *"There is not much wind"* said Captain Smith.
> *"No, it is a flat calm, as a matter of fact"* I replied.
> *"A flat calm. Yes, quite flat"* replied Smith.

> *I said that it was a pity the wind had not kept up with us whilst we were going through the ice region. Of course he knew I meant the water ripples breaking on the base of the berg...I remember saying, 'Of course there will be a certain amount of reflected light*

from the bergs.' with which the Captain agreed. Even with the blue side toward us, we both
agreed that there would still be the white outline.

■ **9:00 p.m.:** Captain Smith updated the chart to reflect the 7:30 position fix Lightoller had taken. This should have allowed Smith to see the location of the ice field that *Titanic* was rapidly approaching.

■ **9:30 p.m.:** Captain Smith retired to his cabin, telling Lightoller "If it becomes at all doubtful let me know at once. I shall be just inside."

■ **9:30 p.m.:** Lightoller sent a message to the crow's nest to keep a sharp lookout for ice. It was now about the time that Lightoller figured they would be entering the area of the icefield.

■ **9:40 p.m.:** Message received by Jack Phillips in the wireless room: *"From Mesaba to Titanic. In latitude 42° N to 41° 25', longitude 49° W to longitude 50° 30' W, saw much heavy pack ice and great number large icebergs, also field ice, weather good, clear."*
This message did not get delivered to the bridge. Phillips was working alone because Bride had gone to bed to rest for awhile before he relieved Phillips at midnight. *Titanic* had just recently come within range of the Cape Race land station and Phillips was extremely busy with all of the commercial traffic to be sent them. The message was laid on a desk by the door of the wireless office and a weight was placed on top of it to keep it from going astray.
Unfortunately, *Titanic* was already inside the area described in *Mesaba's* message, and Captain Smith knew nothing about it.

■ **10:00 p.m.:** Murdoch replaced Lightoller on the bridge for the next four-hour watch. Before returning to his cabin to sleep, Lightoller made his rounds through the ship. He observed that the temperature was continuing to drop and it was now 31 degrees. Down in the First Class Lounge, he found many of the passengers listening to Wallace Hartley and the orchestra while others were engrossed in one of the several card games.

■ **10:00 p.m.:** High up in the crow's nest on the fore mast, lookouts Frederick Fleet and Reginald Lee replaced George Symons and Archie Jewell. Word was passed to Fleet and Lee to watch for icebergs.
The crow's nest was an open platform, exposed to the wind and cold. The air temperature by this time had dropped to 31 degrees and, combined with the 22.5 knot speed of the ship, the lookouts had a real problem keeping their eyes open as the cold air stung and burned them. Fleet

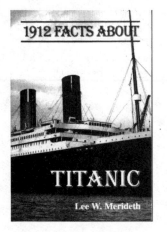